W9-AXC-278

Properties of
Atoms &
Molecules

1:1
Answers
IN GENESIS™

GOD'S
DESIGN®

4th Edition
by Debbie & Richard Lawrence

God's Design® for Chemistry and Ecology is a complete chemistry and ecology curriculum for grades 3–8. The books in this series are designed for use in the Christian school and homeschool, and provide easy-to-use lessons that will encourage children to see God's hand in everything around them.

Printed January 2016

Fourth edition. Copyright © 2003, 2008, 2016 by Debbie & Richard Lawrence.

ISBN: 978-1-62691-471-1

Published by Answers in Genesis, 2800 Bullittsburg Church Rd., Petersburg KY 41080

Book designer: Diane King
Editor: Gary Vaterlaus

The publisher and authors have made every reasonable effort to ensure that the activities recommended in this book are safe when performed as instructed but assume no responsibility for any damage caused or sustained while conducting the experiments and activities. It is the parents', guardians', and/or teachers' responsibility to supervise all recommended activities.

Printed in China

AnswersInGenesis.org • GodsDesign.com

Welcome to GOD'S DESIGN®

CHEMISTRY & ECOLOGY

You are about to start an exciting series of lessons on chemistry and ecology. *God's Design® for Chemistry & Ecology* consists of three books: *Properties of Atoms & Molecules*, *Properties of Matter*, and *Properties of Ecosystems*. Each of these books will give you insight into how God designed and created our world and the universe in which we live.

No matter what grade you are in, third through eighth grade, you can use this book.

3rd–5th grade

Read the lesson.

 Do the activity in the light blue box (worksheets will be provided by your teacher).

 Test your knowledge by answering the **What did we learn?** questions.

 Assess your understanding by answering the **Taking it further** questions.

Be sure to read the special features and do the final project.

There are also unit quizzes and a final test to take.

6th–8th grade

Read the lesson.

 Do the activity in the light blue box (worksheets will be provided by your teacher).

 Test your knowledge by answering the **What did we learn?** questions.

 Assess your understanding by answering the **Taking it further** questions.

 Do the Challenge section in the light green box. This part of the lesson will challenge you to do more advanced activities and learn additional interesting information.

Be sure to read the special features and do the final project.

There are also unit quizzes and a final test to take.

When you truly understand how God has designed everything in our universe to work together, then you will enjoy the world around you even more. So let's get started!

UNIT 1

Atoms & Molecules

◊ **Identify** and **describe** the parts of an atom using diagrams.

◊ **Use** the periodic table to determine the characteristics of atoms.

◊ **Describe** the relationship between atoms and molecules.

1

Introduction to Chemistry

The study of matter and molecules

What is chemistry?

Words to know:

chemistry   chemist

matter

Chemistry may sound like a big word and a difficult subject to study, but it's not. **Chemistry** is simply the study of matter, and **matter** is anything that has mass and takes up space. Some examples of matter are water, wood, air, food, paper, your pet skunk, or your little brother. So if you are interested in learning more about anything around you, then you are ready to learn about chemistry.

Chemists are scientists who study what things are made of, how they react to each other, and how they react to their environment. Chemistry is the study of the basic building blocks of life and the world.

In chemistry you will learn about atoms and molecules. You will learn about how substances combine to make other substances. You will find out how a substance changes form and you will discover that God created our world with such intricate

designs that we may never fully understand how everything works.

God has established laws that govern how chemicals react and how matter changes. Many of these laws seem mysterious because they happen on an atomic level. Although these changes cannot be seen with the naked eye, the results of these laws can be seen all around us. As you study atoms and molecules you will begin to understand these laws and appreciate the beauty of God's design on the atomic level. ✳

🧠 What did we learn?

- What is matter?
- Does air have mass?
- What do chemists study?

🚀 Taking it further

- Would you expect to see the same reaction each time you combine baking soda and vinegar?

Chemistry is fun

As you will learn in the upcoming lessons, some materials are very stable and do not change easily. Other materials are very reactive and easily combine with other substances to make a new substance.

Purpose: To see a chemical reaction

Materials: baking soda, drinking cup, vinegar

Procedure:

1. Place 1 teaspoon of baking soda in a drinking cup.

2. Pour 1 tablespoon of vinegar into the cup. Now watch the reaction!

Conclusion: Vinegar is an acid and baking soda is a base. Acids and bases easily combine together to form salts. In this reaction they also produce a gas. Can you guess what that gas might be? It is carbon dioxide.

Soda fountain

For an even more impressive reaction, you can make a Mentos and diet soda fountain. This chemical reaction is very messy so this experiment must be done outside. This experiment happens quickly so you want to have everything ready before you start. Read through the directions below before you try the experiment so you know what to do.

Purpose: To make a diet soda fountain

Materials: 2-liter bottle of diet cola, heavy paper, tape, toothpick, Mentos® mints

Procedure:

1. Remove the cap from a 2-liter bottle of diet cola.

2. Make a tube to hold the mints: roll a piece of heavy paper into a tube that just fits around the mouth of the soda bottle. Tape the paper so it stays rolled up.

3. Use a toothpick to punch holes through the bottom of the tube just above the mouth of the bottle so that the toothpick goes through the tube and holds the mints in place.

4. Load up your tube with four or more mints.

5. Quickly remove the toothpick and step back so you don't get sprayed. You should see a fountain of soda. Be sure to clean up your mess when you are done.

Conclusion: This reaction is partially a chemical reaction and partially a physical reaction between the mints and the soda. Soda contains a gas called carbon dioxide. This gas is trapped between the liquid molecules. The mints have many tiny pits on their surfaces which allows the gas to collect very quickly and escape the liquid. There is also a chemical reaction between the mints and soda that further allows the gas to escape quickly producing a fountain of foam. Now, don't you think chemistry is fun?

Atoms

Basic building blocks

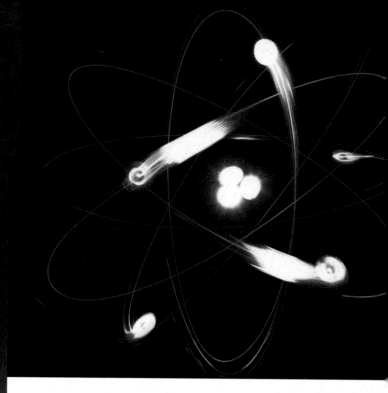

What are the basic building blocks of matter?

Words to know:

atom	nucleus
proton	electron energy level
neutron	valence electron
electron	

Everything around you is made of matter. But what is matter made of? This is a question that has interested scientists for thousands of years. It is obvious that water is a different kind of substance than a rock and that a person is very different from a tree. But what makes each thing unique? As scientists considered this question, they began to try to separate and break down different substances to understand what they were made of. Eventually, scientists have discovered that everything in the universe is made of very small particles called atoms. **Atoms** are the smallest part of matter that cannot be broken down by ordinary chemical means. Atoms are so small that we cannot see them, even with the best microscope. But we can see how different types of atoms behave and see how they combine with other atoms.

Because atoms are so small, scientists have had to develop models to describe what an atom is like. Have you every played with a toy truck or airplane? That toy was a model of the real thing. It allowed you to see the basic parts of the vehicle, but it was not the same size or as complex as the real thing. In the same way, models of atoms help us to understand the basic parts of an atom, but they are not the same size or as complex as a real atom.

The earliest written ideas showing that matter was made of atoms come from the Greeks around 400 BC. The Greek scientists believed that matter was made of very small particles. But they did not try to describe those particles. Work on an actual atomic model did not really begin until the 1700s when experimental science became more popular. Early experiments showed that different atoms had different masses. In 1897 it was discovered that atoms consisted of electrically charged particles and

Fun Fact

The models used to represent atoms do not accurately show the size relationship between the nucleus and the electrons. If the nucleus of the atom was the size of a tennis ball, the electrons would be orbiting about 1 mile away.

Neils Bohr

Ernest Rutherford

that some particles in the atom were smaller than others. By 1911 a scientist named Ernest Rutherford discovered that atoms consisted of a positively-charged nucleus with negatively-charged particles whirling around it. And finally, Neils Bohr discovered that the electrons whirling around the nucleus had different energy levels.

All of these discoveries have helped in the development of the current atomic model. Today scientists describe an atom as having three parts: protons, neutrons, and electrons. **Protons** are positively charged particles. **Neutrons** are neutral; they do not have a positive or negative charge. And **electrons** are negatively charged particles. All of the parts of an atom are extremely small; however, electrons are much smaller than protons and neutrons. Protons and neutrons are approximately 1,800 times more massive than electrons.

The protons and neutrons in an atom are combined together in a tight mass called the **nucleus**. The electrons move very quickly around the nucleus. Some electrons orbit more closely to the nucleus than others. It is believed that the electrons in an atom occupy different levels, or distances, from the nucleus depending on how much energy they have. These levels are often referred to as the **electron energy levels**. The electrons that are in the level farthest away from the nucleus are called the **valence electrons**.

The model of a lithium atom below shows its nucleus containing four neutrons and three protons. It also shows three electrons orbiting the nucleus. Two electrons orbit closer to the nucleus, and the third electron orbits farther away, thus lithium has one valence electron.

The number of protons in the nucleus of an atom determines what kind of atom it is. If an atom loses or gains a neutron, or loses or gains an electron, it is still the same type of atom. But if the atom loses or gains a proton, it becomes a different type of material. Regardless of the number of neutrons or electrons that a lithium atom may have, a lithium atom always has three protons.

As research into the structure of atoms continues, scientists continue to gain more understanding of the complexity of the atom. It is believed that protons, neutrons, and electrons are made of smaller particles called quarks, but because of their extremely small size, they are difficult to study. This complexity continues to amaze scientists and shows God's mighty hand in the design of the universe. ✳

What did we learn?

- What is an atom?
- What are the three parts of an atom?
- What electrical charge does each part of the atom have?
- What is the nucleus of an atom?
- What part of the atom determines what type of atom it is?
- What is a valence electron?

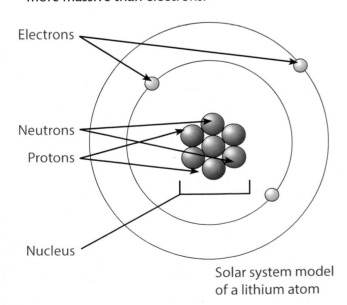

Electrons

Neutrons

Protons

Nucleus

Solar system model of a lithium atom

Taking it further

- Why is it necessary to use a model to show what an atom is like?

- On your worksheet, you colored neutrons blue and protons red. Are neutrons actually blue and protons actually red in a real atom?

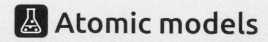 # Atomic models

Color the parts of the atoms on the "Atomic Models" worksheet.

Energy levels

In all atoms, the lowest electron energy level, that which is closest to the nucleus, is filled with electrons first. If a level is full, electrons will occupy the next level. The first level can hold up to two electrons. If an atom has more than two electrons, two electrons will orbit close to the nucleus, and the others will begin to fill the next layer. The following chart shows how many electrons scientists believe that each energy level can hold. Note, however, that although scientists believe that certain levels can hold more electrons, the highest number of electrons that has been determined to be in any energy level is 32. Other than in level one, an inner energy level does not have to be full before the next level begins to fill up. For example, even though the fourth level can hold 32 electrons, the fifth level begins filling up after the fourth level has only 8 electrons in it.

The electrons orbiting in the energy level farthest from the nucleus of an atom are called valence electrons. The lithium model on the previous page shows that lithium has one valence electron. Valence electrons play a vital role in how an element behaves. Neutral atoms are ones in which the number of electrons equals the number of protons. However, atoms can gain or lose valence electrons. The ability to gain, lose, or share valence electrons is what allows atoms to bond with each other to form new substances.

Look at the periodic table of the elements on page 24. The small numbers in the bottom of each box show the electron configuration for each element. For example, look at the box for lithium (Li), element

number 3. The numbers at the bottom of the box are 2, 1. This means there are 2 electrons in the first energy level and 1 electron in the second energy level. This corresponds to the model earlier in this lesson.

Let's look at another example. Look at Potassium (K), which is element number 19. The numbers for the electron configuration are 2, 8, 8, 1. This means that there are 2 electrons orbiting close to the nucleus. There are 8 electrons orbiting in the next level out. There are 8 electrons orbiting in the third level out, and there is 1 electron in the outermost layer. We will learn more about why these electron configurations are so important as we learn about how atoms bond with each other.

Complete the "Energy Levels" worksheet to help you better understand how electrons are distributed in atoms.

Chart of Maximum Electrons in Each Energy Level

Energy Level	Maximum Number of Electrons
1	2
2	8
3	18
4	32
5	50
6	72
7	98

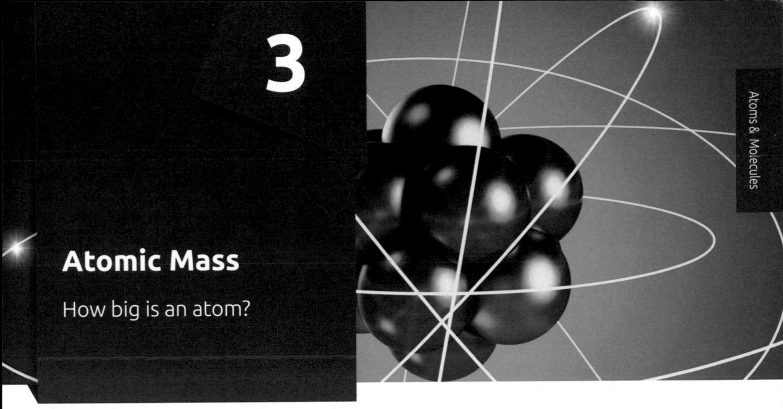

3

Atomic Mass

How big is an atom?

How do you measure an atom's mass?

Words to know:

atomic number

mass number

atomic mass

atomic mass unit (amu)

Challenge words:

isotope

As you learned in the previous lesson, an atom consists of three parts: protons, neutrons, and electrons. You also learned that the number of protons determines the type of element the atom will be. Therefore, the number of protons in an atom is called the **atomic number**. Hydrogen, which only has one proton, has an atomic number of 1. Oxygen, which has eight protons in its nucleus, has an atomic number of 8. The atomic number of an atom is very useful in identifying the type of atom.

The number of electrons in an atom typically equals the number of protons. However, an atom may lose or gain electrons. When this happens it is called an ion. You'll learn about ions in Lesson 11.

The mass of an atom is also an important characteristic to know about the atom. The mass of

an atom is determined by the number of protons and neutrons in the atom. Electrons are so small and contribute such a tiny amount to the mass that their mass can be ignored. The **mass number** or **atomic mass** of an element is found by adding the number of protons and the number of neutrons in the atom. For example, hydrogen has only one proton and no neutrons so its atomic mass is one. Oxygen, which usually has eight protons and eight neutrons, has an atomic mass of 16.

On the other hand, if you are given the atomic number and atomic mass for an element you can figure out how many protons, electrons, and neutrons that element has. The atomic number given at the top of the square on a periodic table tells you how many protons the element has. The number of electrons is equal to the number of protons. Then to calculate the number of neutrons you subtract the number of protons from the atomic mass.

Because the mass of a proton or neutron is so small, it would not make sense to measure an atom's mass in grams. Therefore a special unit has been defined for measuring the mass of an atom. This unit is an **atomic mass unit**, or **amu** (it is also called *unified atomic mass unit* and abbreviated as u). An amu is defined as $\frac{1}{12}$ the mass of a carbon atom. A carbon atom has six protons and six neutrons, and thus has an atomic mass of 12 amu.

Protons and neutrons have nearly identical masses, so for most applications an amu can be used to describe the mass of either type of particle. The mass of an electron is 1,800 times smaller than that of a proton or neutron, so we usually say its mass is negligible—it can be ignored. ✳

What did we learn?

- What are the three particles that make up an atom?

- What is the atomic number of an atom?

- What is the atomic mass of an atom?

- How can you determine the number of electrons, protons, and neutrons in an atom if you are given the atomic number and atomic mass?

Taking it further

- What does a hydrogen atom become if it loses its electron?

- Why are electrons ignored when calculating an element's mass?

Learning about atoms

Complete the "Learning About Atoms" worksheet.

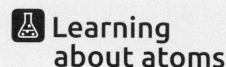

Isotopes

If you look up the atomic mass for an element on the periodic table, you find that most are not listed as whole numbers. This does not mean that an atom has only part of a proton or part of a neutron. It means that even though all atoms of a particular element have the same number of protons, some have different numbers of neutrons. Each variety of atom is called an **isotope** of that element.

To help you understand this better, let's look at carbon. On most periodic tables, the atomic mass of carbon is listed as 12.01 amu. This is an average mass for carbon atoms that naturally occur. All carbon atoms have 6 protons or they would not be carbon atoms. Ninety-nine percent of all carbon atoms also have 6 neutrons giving them a mass of 12 amu. However, a little less than 1% of all carbon atoms have 7 neutrons so they have a mass of 13 amu; and a very

small percentage of carbon atoms have 8 neutrons and a mass of 14 amu. When you average the mass for all isotopes of carbon the average mass is 12.01 amu. Some elements have only a few known isotopes while others have many. Chlorine has 24 known isotopes, but only two are common. The most common has an atomic mass of 35 amu, and the second most common has a mass of 37 amu.

Now that you have a better understanding of what atomic number, atomic mass, and isotopes mean, use a periodic table to fill in the "Understanding Atoms" worksheet. Round the atomic mass from the periodic table to find the most common number of neutrons, in other words the most common isotope, for each element. You may use the periodic table on page 24.

Madame Curie

1867–1934

Atoms, isotopes, and radioactive decay are the things that Marie Curie is best known for. But who was she? When she was born in 1867, her last name was Sklodowska. She was born in Warsaw, Poland, an area that was controlled by the czar of Russia at that time. Because of their pro-Polish leanings, Marie's parents lost their jobs and her father was forced into a series of lower academic posts. The family was poor and took in students as boarders to help pay the rent. When Marie was eight, her oldest sister died, and less than three years later her mother also died. This made the family turn to each other for strength.

As they were growing up, their father read them classics and exposed them to science. Marie graduated from high school at the age of 15, at the top of her class. But, women were not allowed to attend the University of Warsaw, so Marie went to a floating university, named so because it changed locations frequently to hide it from the Russian authorities. This schooling was not a high quality education, so Marie made a pact with her older sister. Marie would work and help send her sister to Paris for medical school, and then her sister would work to send her to school. For two years, Marie worked as a teacher and then, to make more money, she became a governess and sent as much money as she could to her sister.

Eventually, Marie went back home and because of her father's new job she was able to leave for Paris in 1891, when she was 24 years old. There, life was hard for her. In the winters, she would wear every piece of clothing she had to keep herself warm. And sometimes she would get so absorbed in her studies she would forget to eat and she would pass out. In later years, Marie said it was very common for the Polish students to be poor.

In Paris, Marie found that she was ill prepared for college. She was lacking in both math and

science, plus her technical French was behind where it needed to be. She overcame this by working hard, and it paid off. She finished first in her class for her master's degree in physics and second in her class in math the following year.

In 1894 Marie began sharing lab space with a man named Pierre Curie. Their work drew them together, and in July 1895 the two were married in a simple ceremony. In September of 1897 their first child was born—a baby girl. Pierre's father delivered the baby. A few weeks later Pierre's mother died and Pierre's father, along with Marie, Pierre, and baby Irene moved into a house together. Marie kept working in the lab and found her father-in-law to be the perfect babysitter.

About six months after Marie and Pierre were married, a German scientist name Wilhelm Conrad Roentgen discovered X-rays. He discovered that X-rays could travel through wood and flesh and produce an image on photographic paper. A few months later a French physicist named Henri Becquerel discovered that uranium produced similar rays.

These discoveries prompted Marie and Pierre to start working with uranium. They soon discovered other materials that also emitted strong rays and they called this characteristic *radioactivity*. One element they discovered was polonium, named for Marie's home country of Poland, but the most important radioactive material discovered by the Curies was radium. It wasn't long before radium was in demand. In cheap novels, it was touted as "a magical substance whose rays could cure all ills, power wondrous machines, or destroy a city at one blow." This obviously was quite an exaggeration; however, the damaging effects radioactivity has on tissues was soon used on cancer cells. These damaging effects also took their toll on both Marie and her husband. Pierre developed sores on his body and was constantly fatigued. Marie lost 20 pounds and her fingertips were scarred from the radiation, but they had no knowledge of the long-term effects. While they noted Pierre's loss of good health and the severe pains he experienced, they did not link this to their work.

In 1903 both Pierre and Marie were invited to England to be honored for their work at the Royal Institution. Because it was not customary for women to speak there, Lord Kelvin showed his support for Marie by sitting next to her as her husband gave his speech. Later, when Pierre was nominated for the Nobel Prize in Physics for his and Marie's discovery of radium, he said it would be a travesty if his wife was not also included; so she was. In 1911 Marie received a second Nobel Prize, this one in chemistry, for the discovery of the atomic mass of radium.

After Pierre was killed by a horse-drawn wagon in 1906, Marie continued to carry on their work. A little while later, she was offered and accepted her husband's academic post at the Sorbonne, becoming the first woman to teach at this prestigious French college. Over the next few years, with the help of some wealthy friends and the French government, she was able to found the Radium Institute where research into the uses of radium in treating cancer and other illnesses was to be conducted.

When war came to France in 1914, the Radium Institute was complete, but Marie had not moved in yet. The other researchers who worked there were drafted to fight the Germans, and Marie also wanted to help. She knew X-rays could help save soldiers' lives by showing the doctors where the bullets or shrapnel were located, and they could see how the bones were broken. So she helped design 20 radiology vans to be taken into the field to treat the wounded. Since no one else was trained to use the X-ray equipment, Marie learned how to drive and she and her very mature 17 year old daughter, along with a doctor, made the first trip to the front lines in the fall of 1914. By 1916 Marie was training other women to work in the 20 mobile units and at the 200 stationary units.

After the war, Marie went back to work at the Radium Institute, and between 1919 and her death from leukemia in 1934, the Institute published 483 works, including 31 papers and books by Marie. Both of her daughters also achieved distinction. Irene and her husband won a Nobel Prize, and her daughter Eve was recognized for her writings. But the Curies will continue to be best known for their discovery of radioactivity.

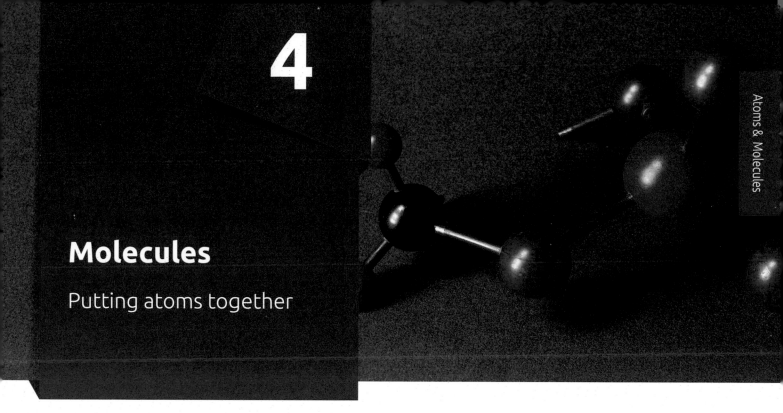

4

Molecules

Putting atoms together

How do atoms combine?

Words to know:

molecule   compound

diatomic molecule

Atoms seldom exist by themselves. Instead, most atoms bond with other atoms. A group of chemically connected atoms is called a **molecule**. How atoms will connect with each other is determined by the number of valence electrons each atom has. Atoms do not usually react if they have eight valence electrons. This is considered a full outer layer and the atom will be stable and unlikely to bond with other atoms. There are only six elements that naturally have eight valence electrons and are thus stable by themselves. All other atoms will try to combine with other atoms to create a full outer layer of electrons.

Some atoms combine with other atoms of the same element. For example, oxygen atoms are seldom found by themselves. Instead, two oxygen atoms usually combine together. When two atoms of the same material combine to form a molecule the result is called a **diatomic** (meaning *two atoms*) **molecule.** Oxygen is the most common diatomic

molecule, but several other gases exist as diatomic molecules as well, including hydrogen, nitrogen, and fluorine.

When atoms of different elements combine together to form a molecule, it is called a **compound.** The most common compound on earth is water, which is a combination of two hydrogen atoms and one oxygen atom. God has created the elements in such a way that multiple atoms can combine together in nearly innumerable ways. So far, over three million compounds have been identified.

When atoms combine to form compounds, the new substance that is formed has completely different characteristics from the elements that form it. For example, sugar is formed from carbon, hydrogen,

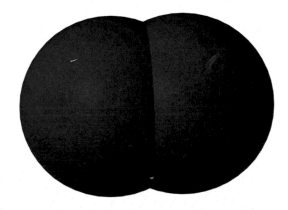

A model of the diatomic molecule dinitrogen, N_2

🧪 Understanding molecules

To help you better understand the differences between atoms, diatomic molecules, and compounds, complete the "What Am I?" worksheet.

and oxygen atoms. Yet the sweet compound we use in so many baked goods has no resemblance to carbon, which is what diamonds are made of, or hydrogen or oxygen, which are both colorless gases.

It is also important to understand the same groups of elements can combine in different amounts to form different substances. For example, if two hydrogen atoms and one oxygen atom combine they form water. But if two hydrogen atoms and two oxygen atoms combine together, they form hydrogen peroxide, which is a clear liquid, but is very different from water. Similarly six carbon atoms, twelve hydrogen atoms, and six oxygen atoms can combine together to form glucose which is a simple sugar. But if only one carbon atom, two hydrogen atoms, and one oxygen atom combine together it forms formaldehyde, which is a substance used to preserve dead animals. So you can see that even though the same types of atoms combine together, they form very different substances if the numbers of atoms are different. ✳

Sugar is formed from carbon, hydrogen, and oxygen, yet it bares no resemblance to carbon.

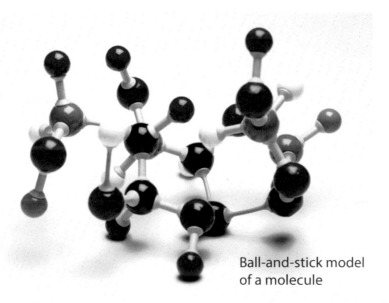

Ball-and-stick model of a molecule

🧠 What did we learn?

- What is a molecule?
- What is a diatomic molecule?
- What is a compound?

🚀 Taking it further

- What is the most important factor in determining if two atoms will bond with each other?
- Table salt is a compound formed from sodium and chlorine. Would you expect sodium atoms and chlorine atoms to taste salty? Why or why not?

🏅 Molecule puzzle pieces

Atoms bond together primarily based on the configuration of their valence electrons. Atoms like to have eight electrons in their outermost layer. So an atom with six valence electrons will bond easily with an atom with two valence electrons. It will also bond with two atoms that each have one valence electron. This is why water is made up of one oxygen atom, which has six valence electrons, and two hydrogen atoms which each have one electron. Together they make eight electrons in the outermost layer.

Check your understanding of this idea by using the "Molecule Puzzle Pieces" to try to form molecules.

Cut out each piece of the "Molecule Puzzle Pieces" worksheet. The dots on each piece represent the number of valence electrons that each element has. For example, the oxygen piece (O) has six dots because it has six valence electrons and the sodium piece (Na) has only one dot because it has only one valence electron.

Atoms are stable when they have eight valence electrons with the exception of hydrogen and helium. Hydrogen and helium only need two valence electrons to be stable. Try fitting the various pieces together to form stable molecules.

Try the following combinations:

- Two hydrogen pieces together—this forms the diatomic molecule H_2

- Two hydrogen pieces and one oxygen piece—this forms a water molecule

- One sodium and one chlorine—this forms table salt

Neon cannot combine with any of the other pieces because it already has a full set of eight electrons in its outer level. Neon is on the far right side of the periodic table. Elements on the far right side are unlikely to bond with other elements.

UNIT 2

Elements

◊ **Describe** how the periodic table can be used to classify elements.

◊ **Distinguish** between the properties of metals and nonmetals.

◊ **Explain** the importance of hydrogen, carbon, and oxygen.

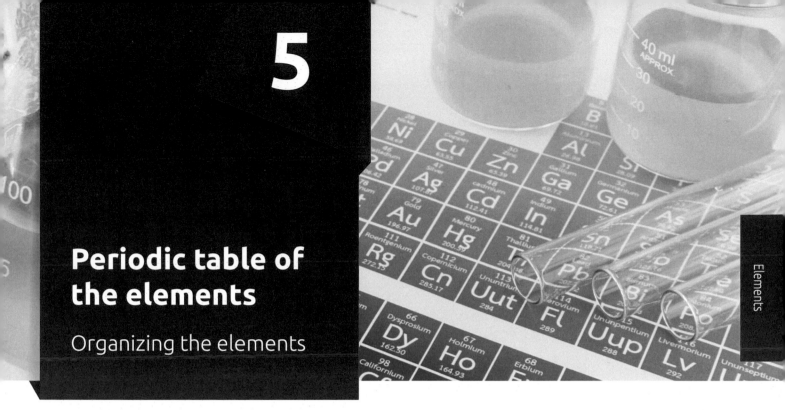

Periodic table of the elements

Organizing the elements

How are elements classified?

Words to know:

transition elements

family

period

There are 98 naturally occurring elements. And scientists have been able to produce another 20 elements in the laboratory. Each of these elements has unique properties. Keeping track of information for all of the elements that have been discovered can be a big task. Fortunately for you, much of that information can be found in a periodic table of the elements. Periodic tables sometimes have additional information, but all periodic tables have at least the following information. Each square will show the name of the element, the symbol for the

Fun Fact

The Latin term for lead is *plumbum*. Because pipes that carried water were originally made of lead or plumbum, the people who installed the pipes were called plumbers.

element, the atomic number, and the atomic mass. Remember that the atomic number is equal to the number of protons in the nucleus and the atomic mass is equal to the average of the number of protons plus the number of neutrons for all isotopes of the element. The symbol is one to three letters derived from the name of the element.

Some of the symbols for the names of the elements are obvious while others may not make much sense to you. It is obvious why hydrogen has the symbol H and oxygen is O. However, what would you expect the symbol to be for lead? Did you think it should be L or Le? That would make sense, but the symbol for lead is Pb. This may seem strange, but the Latin name for lead is *plumbum* so lead is designated at Pb. Several other symbols on the periodic table are also derived from their Latin names, while we are familiar with the English names for those elements. Look at the periodic table and see which other symbols do not match the English version of the element's name. Did you find Na for sodium, K for potassium, Fe for iron, and Au for gold? If you look up the Latin names for these elements you will find that the symbols make more sense.

You know that the periodic table gives information about all of the known elements on earth. Look at the table and try to figure out how the elements are arranged on the table. Some of the arrangement is easy to figure out. It is obvious that the elements are listed in order of their atomic numbers. It starts with number 1 and goes up to number 118. But it might not be as obvious why certain elements are in each column or each row. The arrangement of the electrons in an atom determines which row and which column it will be in.

The elements are put into columns according to the number of electrons in the outermost layer, those that are orbiting farthest away from the nucleus. All of the elements in the first column have one electron in the outer layer. The elements in the second column have two electrons in the outer layer. The columns in the middle are called **transition elements** and have special rules for how they are arranged. These are the elements in the yellow squares below. If you skip over them, to the column labeled IIIA, you find elements that have three electrons in their outermost layer and so on. Elements in a column will react to other elements in a similar way as other elements in that column. The

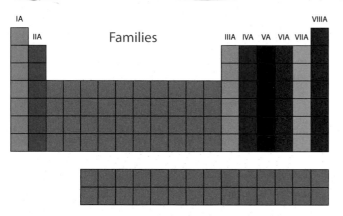

elements in a column are called a **family** or group.

The elements are put into rows according to how many layers of electrons they have. Hydrogen and helium are the only elements in the first row because they are the only elements that have only one layer of electrons. The elements in the second row have two layers of electrons, the elements in the third row have three layers, and so on. Each row

in the periodic table is called a **period**, hence the name periodic table.

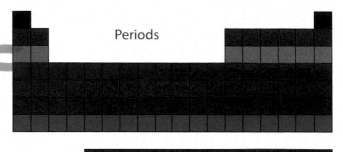

Fun Fact

When lighter-than-air ships were first designed, many were filled with hydrogen. Hydrogen is the lightest known element, thus making the ships float easily. However, after a terrible fire in the *Hindenburg* airship in 1937, it was decided that hydrogen was too dangerous. It was believed at the time that since hydrogen has only one electron and is highly reactive, that the fire was caused by lightning, or some other spark, causing the hydrogen to react with oxygen leading to the tragedy. After this tragic accident, it was decided to change from hydrogen to helium. Helium is a noble gas. It is very stable and does not react easily with other elements, yet it is still much lighter than air and allows blimps to be used in many areas still today.

Many researchers today believe that the fire in the *Hindenburg* was not a result of the hydrogen gas. It is now believed that the aluminum powder varnish used to coat the outside of the ship built up a huge electrostatic charge and caught fire when the electricity was discharged. They believe this fire would have started regardless of the gas used inside the ship.

🧪 Using the periodic table

You will become more comfortable with the periodic table of the elements as you use it more, so now you have a chance to use it. Use the periodic table on page 24 to answer the questions on the "Learning About the Elements" worksheet.

Once you understand more about how the elements are arranged on the periodic table, you will be able to tell a lot about each element just by where it is on the table. ✳

What did we learn?

- How many valence electrons do the elements in each column have?

- What four pieces of information are included for each element in any periodic table of the elements?

- What do all elements in a column on the periodic table have in common?

- What do all elements in a row on the periodic table have in common?

 Taking it further

- Atoms are stable when they have eight electrons in their outermost energy level. Therefore elements from column IA will react easily with elements from which column?

- Elements from column IIA will react easily with elements from which column?

Synthetic elements

Twenty of the elements on the periodic table do not occur naturally; they have only been produced by scientists in a laboratory or as a result of a nuclear explosion. These elements are called synthetic elements. Elements 99–118 are all synthetic. Nine other elements have been discovered in trace amounts in nature but were first observed by scientists who were making elements in a laboratory. All synthetic elements are very unstable. The nucleus of a synthetic element quickly breaks apart in a process called radioactive decay. The time for half of a sample to decay is called the half-life of that element. Synthetic elements have a half-life of between a microsecond and 1 year. Most synthetic elements only exits for a very short period of time.

Synthetic elements are created in one of two ways, either through a nuclear reaction such as a nuclear bomb explosion or in a nuclear reactor, or by experiment using a particle accelerator, which causes atoms to collide with each other at very high speeds. When two atoms collide, sometimes their nuclei fuse together. This forms a new element because the new nucleus now has more protons. Because these elements exist for such a short period of time, it is difficult to verify their existence, and there has been some controversy over whether some elements have actually been discovered or not.

The first element to be created in a laboratory was technetium in 1936. This is element 43 on the periodic table. It was created to fill a hole or space left in the periodic table. Scientists knew that there had

to be an element that fit in that spot on the table, but no one had ever found any naturally occurring. Since that time trace amounts of technetium have been discovered on earth, and it is believed that it exists in larger amounts in red giant stars.

The first truly synthetic elements were discovered in 1952 when scientists were analyzing the results of the detonation of the first hydrogen bomb. Two new elements were discovered and were given the names einsteinium and fermium. They are numbers 99 and 100 on the periodic table. Synthetic elements are usually named for famous scientists or the locations where they were discovered. Although it is believed that elements 113, 115, 117, and 118 have been created, they have not completed the confirmation process and remain officially unnamed.

Naturally occurring elements usually have several different isotopes so the atomic mass listed on the periodic table is an average of these various masses for each element. However, since there are no naturally occurring isotopes for synthetic elements, there is no way to find an average mass. So the mass listed on the periodic table is the mass for the isotope with the longest half-life.

Because synthetic elements do not last very long they do not have any practical uses other than for scientific experimentation. Many other naturally occurring elements, such as technetium, which occur only in trace amounts, also have no commercial or other practical uses.

Periodic Table of the Elements

Legend:
- Alkali metals
- Alkali-earth metals
- Transition metals
- Poor metals
- Metalloids
- Nonmetals
- Noble gases
- Hydrogen nonmetal

Key:
- Atomic number 12
- Symbol ...... Mg
- Atomic Mass 24.31
- Name .... Magnesium
- Electron structure by energy level 2,8,2

	IA	IIA	IIIB	IVB	VB	VIB	VIIB	VIIIB	VIIIB	VIIIB	IB	IIB	IIIA	IVA	VA	VIA	VIIA	VIIIA
1	H																	He
2	3 Li 6.941 Lithium 2,1	4 Be 9.012 Beryllium 2,2											5 B (10.81) Boron 2,3	6 C 12.01 Carbon 2,4	7 N 14.01 Nitrogen 2,5	8 O 16 Oxygen 2,6	9 F 19 Fluorine 2,7	10 Ne
3	11 Na 22.99 Sodium 2,8,1	12 Mg 24.31 Magnesium 2,8,2											13 Al 26.98 Aluminum 2,8,3	14 Si Silicon	15 P 30.97 Phosphorus 2,8,5	16 S 32.07 Sulfur 2,8,6	17 Cl 35.45 Chlorine 2,8,7	18 Ar
4	19 K 39.1 Potassium 2,8,8,1	20 Ca 40.08 Calcium 2,8,8,2	21 Sc 44.96 Scandium 2,8,9,2	22 Ti 47.9 Titanium 2,8,10,2	23 V 50.94 Vanadium 2,8,11,2	24 Cr 52 Chromium 2,8,13,1	25 Mn 54.94 Manganese 2,8,13,2	26 Fe 55.85 Iron 2,8,14,2	27 Co 58.93 Cobalt 2,8,15,2	28 Ni 58.69 Nickel 2,8,16,2	29 Cu 63.55 Copper 2,8,18,1	30 Zn 65.39 Zinc 2,8,18,2	31 Ga 69.72 Gallium 2,8,18,3	32 Ge Germanium	33 As Arsenic	34 Se 78.96 Selenium 2,8,18,6	35 Br 79.9 Bromine 2,8,18,7	36 Kr
5	37 Rb 85.47 Rubidium 2,8,18,8,1	38 Sr 87.62 Strontium 2,8,18,8,2	39 Y 88.91 Yttrium 2,8,18,9,2	40 Zr 91.22 Zirconium 2,8,18,10,2	41 Nb 92.91 Niobium 2,8,18,12,1	42 Mo 95.94 Molybdenum 2,8,18,13,1	43 Tc 99 Technetium 2,8,18,14,1	44 Ru 101.1 Ruthenium 2,8,18,15,1	45 Rh 102.9 Rhodium 2,8,18,16,1	46 Pd 106.4 Palladium 2,8,18,17,1	47 Ag 107.9 Silver 2,8,18,18,1	48 Cd 112.4 Cadmium 2,8,18,18,2	49 In 114.8 Indium 2,8,18,18,3	50 Sn 118.7 Tin 2,8,18,18,4	51 Sb Antimony	52 Te Tellurium	53 I 126.9 Iodine 2,8,18,18,7	54 Xe
6	55 Cs 132.9 Cesium -18,18,8,1	56 Ba 137.3 Barium -18,18,8,2	57 La 138.9 Lanthanum -18,18,9,2	72 Hf 178.5 Hafnium -18,32,10,2	73 Ta 180.9 Tantalum -18,32,11,2	74 W 183.9 Tungsten -18,32,12,2	75 Re 186.2 Rhenium -18,32,13,2	76 Os 190.2 Osmium -18,32,14,2	77 Ir 192.2 Iridium -18,32,15,2	78 Pt 195.1 Platinum -18,32,17,1	79 Au 197 Gold -18,32,18,1	80 Hg 200.5 Mercury -18,32,18,2	81 Tl 204.4 Thallium -18,32,18,3	82 Pb 207.2 Lead -18,32,18,4	83 Bi 209 Bismuth -18,32,18,5	84 Po Polonium	85 At (210) Astatine -18,32,18,7	86 Rn
7	87 Fr (223) Francium -18,32,18,8,1	88 Ra (226) Radium -18,32,18,8,2	89 Ac (227) Actinium -18,32,18,9,2	104 Rf (261) Rutherfordium	105 Db (262) Dubnium	106 Sg 262.94 Seaborgium	107 Bh (264) Bohrium	108 Hs (265) Hassium	109 Mt (266) Meitnerium	110 Ds (271) Darmstadtium	111 Rg (280) Roentgenium	112 Cn (285) Copernicium	113 Uut (284) Ununtrium	114 Fl (289) Flerovium	115 Uup (288) Ununpentium	116 Lv (293) Livermorium	117 Uus (294) Ununseptium	118 Uuo (294) Ununoctium

Lanthanides / Actinides:

58 Ce 140.1 Cerium -18,20,8,2	59 Pr 140.9 Praseodymium -18,21,8,2	60 Nd 144.2 Neodymium -18,22,8,2	61 Pm (145) Promethium -18,23,8,2	62 Sm 150.4 Samarium -18,24,8,2	63 Eu 152 Europium -18,25,8,2	64 Gd 157.3 Gadolinium -18,25,9,2	65 Tb 158.9 Terbium -18,27,8,2	66 Dy 162.5 Dysprosium -18,28,8,2	67 Ho 164.9 Holmium -18,29,8,2	68 Er 167.3 Erbium -18,30,8,2	69 Tm 168.9 Thulium -18,31,8,2	70 Yb 173 Ytterbium -18,32,8,2	71 Lu 175 Lutetium -18,32,9,2
90 Th 232 Thorium -18,32,18,10,2	91 Pa 233 Protactinium -18,32,20,9,2	92 U 238 Uranium -18,32,21,9,2	93 Np (237) Neptunium -18,32,22,9,2	94 Pu (244) Plutonium -18,32,24,8,2	95 Am (243) Americium -18,32,25,8,2	96 Cm (247) Curium -18,32,25,9,2	97 Bk (247) Berkelium -18,32,26,9,2	98 Cf (251) Californium -18,32,28,8,2	99 Es (252) Einsteinium -18,32,29,8,2	100 Fm (257) Fermium -18,32,30,8,2	101 Md (258) Mendelevium -18,32,31,8,2	102 No (259) Nobelium -18,32,32,8,2	103 Lr (262) Lawrencium -18,32,32,9,2

Note: the lowest electron levels are not shown for rows 6 and 7, instead they are indicated by a -, which means 2, 8.

The periodic table of the elements, which is probably the most important tool a chemist has, is a table that lists some of the most important properties known about each element. But like all tools, someone had to invent it. So how did this useful tool come into existence?

In the early 1800s many scientists tried to find relationships between the various elements, but this was a daunting task, somewhat like sorting the pieces of a jigsaw puzzle without knowing what the picture should be. In 1866 an English scientist named John Newlands began sorting the then-known elements according to their atomic masses. He believed that the properties of the elements repeated every eighth element and he called this the law of octaves. However, there were many elements that did not fit into this pattern and eventually it was discarded. Only three years later, in 1869, a Russian chemist named Dmitri Mendeleev came up with what is considered by most people to be the first periodic table of elements.

Dmitri Mendeleev was born in Siberia, Russia, in 1834, and was the youngest of 14 children. About the time Dmitri finished high school, his father died and his mother moved to St. Petersburg, Russia, where she worked hard to earn the money needed to send Dmitri to college. This sacrifice paid off, not only for Dmitri, but also for all scientists to follow.

After college, Mendeleev began to catalog all the data he could find on the 63 elements known at the time. He was sure that the elements had repeating or "periodic" properties. He wrote the properties of each element on a card, and then he arranged the cards according to their similar properties and in

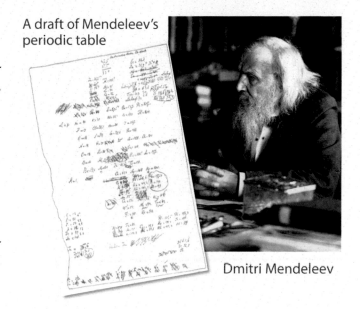

A draft of Mendeleev's periodic table

Dmitri Mendeleev

order of their increasing atomic masses. Mendeleev found that this method worked very well for most elements, and for the few that did not fit, he did a very unusual thing; he moved the element over one space and left a hole. He was convinced that where holes appeared, elements would be found in the future to fill these holes. He was so sure of this that he even predicted what the properties of the elements would be. And over the next several years, these predicted elements were indeed discovered.

The shape of the table has changed several times as scientists have discovered new elements, but the concept developed by Mendeleev has remained the same. The biggest advance to the periodic table after Mendeleev was in 1914, when Henry Moseley decided to arrange the elements according to their atomic numbers instead of their atomic masses. This arrangement solved some of the problems in Mendeleev's table and led to the periodic table we use today.

6

Metals

Silver and gold have I none ...

What are the properties of metals?

Words to know:

malleable
ductile
reactive

metalloid
semiconductor

Challenge words:

noble metals
poor metals

reactivity series

What do you think of when you hear that something is made of metal? Do you think of something hard, heavy, strong, and shiny? That would be a pretty good description of most metals. Do you think of cars, washing machines, silverware, or coins? Those are just a few of the many uses for metal.

Three quarters of all elements on earth are metals. Most are hard, strong, and heavy. However, a few pure metals are weak or soft. The majority of metals have the following six characteristics:

1.   Silvery luster on the surface

2.   Solid at room temperature (except for mercury, which is a liquid)

3.   **Malleable**—can be hammered into shape

4.   **Ductile**—can be drawn into a wire

5.   Good conductor of electricity

6.   Tend to be very **reactive**—easily combines with other elements

Most metals have one to three valence electrons. They easily give up their electrons, which is why they are reactive with many other elements. This is also why metals are good conductors of electricity. Because of their unique characteristics, metals are used in a variety of ways. Their strength and malleability allow them to be used for making cars and trucks, bridges, appliances, aluminum siding, and soda pop cans. Metal's conductivity of electricity is why metal is used for electrical wiring in nearly every house and building in America.

As you go across the periodic table from left to right, the elements become less metallic; this means that they are less malleable, less ductile, and less conductive. The dividing line between the metals and the nonmetals is the diagonal line of elements shaded dark green on the periodic table. These seven elements are called **metalloids**. They act partially

Conducting electricity

Purpose: To demonstrate the electrical conducting ability of metals

Materials: copper wire, flashlight, battery, electrical tape (or duct tape)

Procedure:

1. Cut two 12-inch pieces of copper wire. Strip about 1 inch of plastic off of each end of the wires.

2. Remove the light bulb and battery from a flashlight.

3. Using electrical tape or duct tape, attach one end of a wire to the positive terminal of the battery and the other end of the wire to the side of the metal contact on the light bulb.

4. Tape one end of the second wire to the negative terminal of the battery.

5. Touch the other end of the second wire to the end of the light bulb and watch the bulb light up.

Conclusion: Electrons are flowing from the battery, through the first wire, through the light bulb, through the second wire, and finally back to the battery. Because copper conducts electricity so well, it is used for most electrical wiring in buildings.

like metals and partially like nonmetals. The metalloids are called **semiconductors** because they conduct electricity only under certain circumstances. This is an important characteristic for the technological world. Semiconductors are used to provide low power yet high speed in electronic devices used in many products such as computers, digital watches, and cell phones. ✳

Fun Fact

Manganese is the only metal that is not silvery, ductile, or malleable, which may make it seem like a nonmetal. However, manganese acts like a metal when it is alloyed, or added to other metals.

What did we learn?

- What are the six characteristics of most metals?
- How many valence electrons do most metals have?
- What is a metalloid?

Taking it further

- What are the most likely elements to be used in making computer chips?
- Is arsenic likely to be used as electrical wire in a house?

Reactive metals

Metals can be grouped according to how reactive they are. Based on what you have learned so far, which metals would you expect to be the most reactive? If you said the metals in the first column, you would be correct. The alkali metals are the most reactive metals. Sodium and potassium are both very reactive with air and water as well as other metals. Therefore, they must be stored in oil to keep them from reacting with the air.

The alkali-earth metals, those elements in column IIA, are also highly reactive, but not as reactive as the alkali metals. Because these metals react easily with other metals they readily form compounds. Calcium, one of the alkali-earth metals, is found in large amounts in the crust of the earth in the form of calcite, which is the main ingredient in limestone. Calcium is also found in seashells in the form of calcium carbonate. Alkali metals and alkali-earth metals are seldom found in their pure form because they are so reactive.

All of the metals in the center of the periodic table are called transition metals. Transition metals are what you might consider more typical metals. These are the metals that are used in many of the applications we mentioned earlier in this lesson. A few of the transition metals, those to the far right of the group, including silver, gold, copper, palladium, and platinum are often grouped together as the noble metals. Do you remember which column was called the noble gases? The noble gases are the elements in the far right column. They are the gases that do not easily react with other elements. Similarly, the **noble metals** do not react easily with other metals and are often found in their pure form in the crust of the earth.

Finally, the metals to the right of the transition metals, including aluminum, gallium, indium, tin, antimony, lead, and bismuth are called the **poor metals**. These metals are colored light green on the periodic table in lesson 5. These metals are generally more reactive than the transition metals but less reactive than the alkali and alkali-earth metals. Poor metals are very soft and usually are not very useful by themselves. However, when mixed with other elements, they become very useful.

In order to give people a good idea of how reactive various metals are, scientists have developed the "**Reactivity Series**" which lists a selected group of metals from most reactive to least reactive. This list helps people know what to expect from several common metals when they come in contact with various substances. The most reactive metals will react with water, acids, oxygen and many other substances. These metals are at the top of the list and are found in columns IA and IIA. Metals that react with acids but do not react with water are next on the list. These metals are mostly found in columns IIA, IIIA and IVA. Many of the transition metals (IB – VIIB) react only with oxygen and are near the bottom of the list. Finally, metals that do not easily react with anything (the noble metals) are at the bottom of the list.

Reactivity Series

- Potassium
- Sodium
- Calcium
- Magnesium
- Aluminum
- Zinc
- Iron
- Tin
- Lead
- Copper
- Silver
- Gold
- Platinum

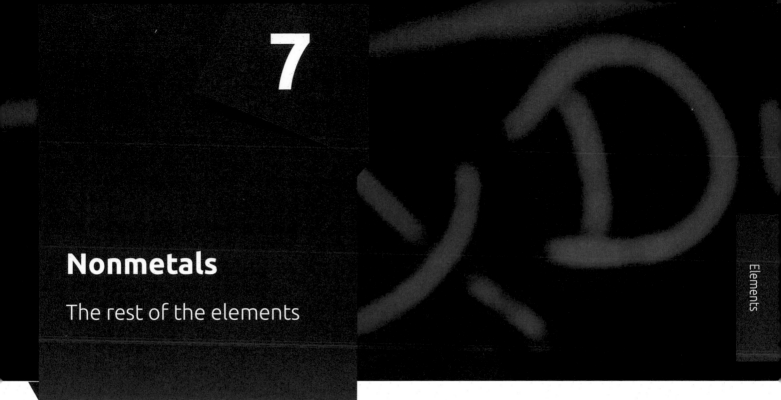

7

Nonmetals

The rest of the elements

What are the properties of nonmetals?

Words to know:

halogens

inert

noble gases

The vast majority of the elements on earth are metals or metalloids. There are only 18 elements that are nonmetals. These include hydrogen, plus the 17 elements to the right of the metalloids. Although hydrogen is listed in the left column of the periodic table because it has only one valence electron, it often acts more like the elements in column VIIA because it only needs one electron to have a full outer shell and is classified as a nonmetal.

Nonmetals have very different characteristics from metals. They generally do not have a silvery luster or shiny appearance. Because the nonmetals need only one to three electrons to fill their outer shells, they do not easily give up electrons but share or gain electrons when they combine with other elements. Because they do not give up electrons, nonmetals are poor conductors of electricity. At room temperature, some nonmetals are solid, some are liquid, but most are gases. Those that are solid are usually brittle and shatter easily.

The top four elements in column VIIA are called **halogens**. These are very reactive elements. These elements can be very dangerous in large quantities, but in small quantities they are very useful. Chlorine is added to drinking water and swimming pools to kill bacteria. Fluorine (in the ionic form of fluoride) is added to drinking water and toothpaste to prevent tooth decay. Iodine can also be used to kill germs and is an essential nutrient in our diets. Because hydrogen is so reactive, it is sometimes grouped with the halogens.

The elements in column VIIIA are called the **noble gases** because they do not easily combine with any other element. Because these elements have eight

Chlorine is added to swimming pools to kill bacteria.

electrons in their outer shells, they are very stable. They are referred to as **inert** gases because they do not react. Their inability to react makes noble gases very useful for certain applications. Noble gases are sometimes used to fill a space instead of air to prevent a reaction from occurring. For example, in the process of making semiconductor chips, the space around the circuitry may be filled with argon gas instead of air to prevent a reaction from occurring.

Noble gases do not easily react with other elements. However, they have another special characteristic that makes them very useful. When a noble gas is in an enclosed container and an electrical current is passed through it, the gas turns into a plasma

The noble gas in a neon sign glows brightly when high voltage is applied.

and a colored light is given off. You have probably seen this phenomenon many times without realizing it. Most of the lighted signs that look like glass

🧪 Protecting your teeth

As we mentioned earlier, fluoride is often added to drinking water and toothpaste to help prevent tooth decay. Fluoride reacts with the calcium in your tooth enamel to make it stronger. The shell of an egg is made of calcium carbonate so it will react with fluoride in a similar way to your teeth. Do the activity below to see how these two elements react with each other. This experiment will take several days.

Purpose: To demonstrate how calcium carbonate and fluoride react together

Materials: fluoride toothpaste, two cups, uncooked egg, nail polish or permanent marker, vinegar

Procedure:

1. Squirt a bunch of fluoride toothpaste into a cup.

2. Make a small mark on one side of an uncooked egg with nail polish or a permanent marker.

3. Push the marked side of the egg into the toothpaste until half of the egg is covered. Let the egg sit in the toothpaste for 3 days.

4. At the end of 3 days, remove the egg and gently wash off the toothpaste and dry the egg.

5. Place the egg in an empty cup.

6. Pour enough vinegar in the cup to completely cover the egg. Observe what happens.

7. Allow the egg to sit in the vinegar for 8 to 12 hours. At the end of this time, carefully remove the egg. It will be very fragile on one side so be very careful.

8. Use a pen to gently tap each side of the egg.

Questions/Conclusion:

- What happened to the egg when you added the vinegar? You should see small bubbles coming off of half the egg shell.

- Did the bubbles form on the half with the mark or on the unmarked half? The bubbles will be forming on the half of the egg that did not have any toothpaste (the unmarked half).

- What do you think is causing the bubbles? Vinegar is an acid. This acid reacts with the calcium in the egg shell and creates carbon dioxide. This is what forms the bubbles. Acid in your mouth reacts with your teeth. If you have acid in your mouth too long, the reaction will make small holes in your teeth. These holes are called cavities.

- When you tapped the egg shell, what did you notice about the difference between the two sides of the egg? The side that soaked in the toothpaste should be much harder than the side that did not have the toothpaste. This is how toothpaste helps to make your teeth stronger so they do not react as easily with the acids in your mouth.

tubes that have been formed into the shape of words or symbols (like the sign on the previous page) are referred to as neon signs. When these tubes are filled with neon gas, the electrical current produces a red/orange colored glow. Not all lighted signs are neon signs. Other noble gases will produce different colors of light. This same trait of inert gases is used in plasma ball toys and plasma TV screens. ✳

 # What did we learn?

- What are some common characteristics of nonmetals?

- What is the most common state, solid, liquid, or gas, for nonmetal elements?
- Why are halogens very reactive?
- Why are noble gases very non-reactive?

 # Taking it further

- Hydrogen often acts like a halogen. How might it act differently from a halogen?
- Why are balloons filled with helium instead of hydrogen?

Incandescent light bulbs

Halogens and noble gases both play important roles in the light bulb industry. A regular incandescent light bulb is a glass bulb with a tungsten filament in the middle. Electricity flows through the filament and heats it up. As it gets hot, as much as 4,500°F (2,500°C), the filament begins to glow and gives off light. Some of the tungsten gets hot enough to evaporate.

The bulb is filled with a noble gas, usually argon. The noble gas prevents the tungsten molecules from reacting with anything, which helps the filament last longer than it would if the bulb were filled with air.

One disadvantage of the incandescent light bulb is that it gives off a large amount of heat as well as light. This is considered an inefficient use of electricity. So scientists have developed other types of light bulbs that give off the same amount of light but use less electricity to do it.

One type of more efficient light bulb is the halogen bulb. A halogen bulb is a special kind of incandescent light bulb that contains a filament surrounded by a small quartz envelope. This envelope is much smaller than the glass bulb of a regular light bulb. Quartz is used because the heat given off by the filament would melt glass.

The envelope is filled with a halogen gas. As you just learned, halogens are very reactive. When the tungsten on the filament vaporizes, it reacts with the halogen gas inside the tube. This new molecule is heavy and falls back onto the filament. The tungsten is then redeposited on the filament. This helps the filament last much longer than it does in a regular

Incandescent, halogen, florescent, and LED bulbs

incandescent light bulb. This design also allows the filament to burn at a much higher temperature, which gives off more light for the amount of electricity. Because it burns at a much higher temperature, a halogen bulb is still very hot, but it lasts much longer than a regular incandescent bulb and produces more light with less electricity.

In this lesson you already learned that noble gases are used in neon lights. And now you know that noble gases and halogen gases are used in incandescent lights as well. The special properties of halogen and noble gases allow us to see in the dark. However, incandescent lights turn most of the energy they use into heat rather than light so other sources of light have been developed. Mercury vapor is used in fluorescent lights, and semi-conducting materials are used in LED lights to provide more efficient and longer lasting light bulbs. By understanding the various properties of the different elements, scientists are able to find just the right material for each purpose.

8

Hydrogen

Very reactive

What is special about hydrogen?

Words to know:

reduction   dehydrogenation

hydrogenation

Challenge words:

hydrogen fuel cell

It's the first element listed in the periodic table and it's the smallest and simplest atom. What is it? It's hydrogen. Hydrogen has an atomic number of 1 because it has one proton and no neutrons in its nucleus. It has one electron in orbit around the nucleus. This is the simplest possible atom. Hydrogen needs only two electrons to make it stable, and since it already has one, it needs only one more. Therefore, hydrogen is often classified as a halogen, because it reacts like a halogen. However, hydrogen can also give up one electron, so it sometimes acts like an alkali metal.

Hydrogen is the lightest element in the universe. If you had a swimming pool full of hydrogen, all the molecules together would only weigh about two pounds. Hydrogen has no smell, taste, or color.

At normal room temperature and pressure, hydrogen is a gas. Hydrogen's boiling point is -423.17°F (-252.87°C) and its freezing point is -434.45°F (-259.14°C).

Hydrogen is the most abundant element in the universe. Hydrogen is believed to be the main element comprising the sun, as well as Jupiter and Saturn. Nearly 90% of all atoms in the universe are believed to be hydrogen atoms. Yet on earth, hydrogen is only the tenth most abundant element. God made the earth different from other planets, with additional elements necessary for life being more abundant than hydrogen.

Most of the hydrogen on earth does not exist as hydrogen gas. Most of the hydrogen is combined with other elements to form compounds. The most common compound containing hydrogen is water. Hydrogen is also found in sugars, amino acids, proteins, cellulose, and fossil fuels such as oil and gasoline. And hydrogen can combine with nitrogen to form ammonia.

Fun Fact

About 1 out of every 6,000 hydrogen atoms has a neutron in its nucleus.

Because hydrogen is so reactive it has many uses. It combines explosively to form water, H_2O. This makes liquid hydrogen and liquid oxygen ideal as rocket fuel. Hydrogen is also being explored as an alternative form of energy for cars. Some hybrid cars now have engines that can use either compressed hydrogen or gasoline to power them.

Hydrogen is used in many chemical processes as well. Hydrogen can be used to remove oxygen from metal oxide ores in a process called **reduction**. A process called **hydrogenation** forces hydrogen molecules through a substance to change its molecular structure. For example, vegetable oil is hydrogenated to become margarine and crude oil is hydrogenated to produce gasoline. **Dehydrogenation** is the process that removes hydrogen atoms from a substance. ✳

 # What did we learn?

- What is the most common element in the universe?
- What is the atomic structure of hydrogen?
- What is the atomic number for hydrogen?
- Why is hydrogen sometimes grouped with the alkali metals?
- Why is hydrogen sometimes grouped with the halogens?

 # Taking it further

- Why is hydrogen one of the most reactive elements?
- Margarine contains only partially hydrogenated oil. What do you suppose fully hydrogenated oils are like?

 # Hydrogenation

Hydrogenation is a process where hydrogen is added to vegetable oil at high temperature, forcing the hydrogen to bond with the oil molecules. This process causes the oil to become thicker. This allows vegetable oil to become margarine. When peanut butter is hydrogenated the peanut oil stays mixed into the peanut butter. Hydrogenated or partially hydrogenated foods are very common.

Purpose: To see which foods contain hydrogenated products

Materials: vegetable oil, margarine, peanut butter, crackers, cookies, dry soup, other pre-packaged meals

Procedure:

1. Read the list of ingredients for vegetable oil, margarine, and peanut butter.

2. Compare the thickness of each of these substances. How does the thickness of the margarine and the peanut butter compare to that of the oil? Which products are hydrogenated?

3. Look at other food labels for hydrogenated oils. You may be surprised at how many products have these substances. Possible places to look include crackers, cookies and other snack foods, dry noodle soups, and many pre-packaged meals.

🏅 Hydrogen fuel cells

Hydrogen plays a vital role in society today, but it is likely to become even more important in the future. Today nearly all vehicles are powered by gasoline or diesel fuel, both of which come from petroleum. However, **hydrogen fuel cells** are being developed, which could power these vehicles using hydrogen instead of gasoline.

Hydrogen fuel cells combine hydrogen gas and oxygen gas to form water. This process releases electricity, which is used to power an electrical motor in the vehicle. This process has many advantages over the current gasoline engine. It produces less air pollution and reduces dependence on foreign oil. It is likely that cars in the future may use this type of technology.

Today there are several obstacles to switching from gasoline to hydrogen. First, there needs to be a cost effective way to obtain the hydrogen. We can't just go find a pocket of hydrogen in the ground and pump it out like we do petroleum for gasoline.

Hydrogen is very reactive and is almost always chemically bonded with other elements. Therefore, the hydrogen must be separated from the other atoms before it can be used to power vehicles.

Second, there needs to be a system set up for drivers to get more hydrogen when they are traveling. Now, a driver can fill up his gas tank nearly anywhere, but there are few hydrogen stations available.

Third, hydrogen is difficult to store and transport. Hydrogen is very light and very small so it must be stored in a container that will keep it from escaping. Also, it must be compressed or cooled so that a large amount will fit in a small space inside the car.

As scientists and engineers work on these problems, it is likely that hydrogen fuel cell cars will become more readily available in the future. To learn more about how hydrogen fuel cells work, visit How Stuff Works or other Internet sites on hydrogen fuel cells.

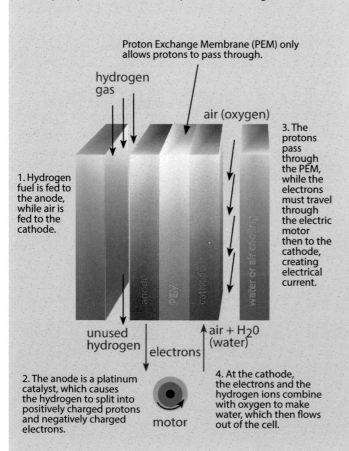

Proton Exchange Membrane (PEM) only allows protons to pass through.

hydrogen gas

air (oxygen)

1. Hydrogen fuel is fed to the anode, while air is fed to the cathode.

3. The protons pass through the PEM, while the electrons must travel through the electric motor then to the cathode, creating electrical current.

unused hydrogen

electrons

air + H_2O (water)

2. The anode is a platinum catalyst, which causes the hydrogen to split into positively charged protons and negatively charged electrons.

motor

4. At the cathode, the electrons and the hydrogen ions combine with oxygen to make water, which then flows out of the cell.

A London bus that runs on hydrogen fuel cells

Carbon

Graphite and diamonds

Elements

What is special about carbon?

Words to know:

carbon cycle

Challenge words:

allotrope   nanotechnology

buckminsterfullerene   carbon nanotubes

buckyballs

Carbon is one of the most important and interesting elements on earth. It can exist as a soft slippery powder called graphite. It can also be found in the form of a diamond, which is the hardest substance on earth. How can the same atoms form such very different substances? It depends on how the atoms are arranged. The carbon atoms in graphite line up in long chains that easily slip over each other. But the carbon atoms in diamond are arranged in a lattice network or crystalline structure that holds each atom tightly in place (see the diagrams later in this lesson). How the carbon atoms line up is greatly affected by temperature and pressure.

The atomic number of carbon is 6. Carbon has six protons and usually has six neutrons in its nucleus.

It also has six electrons. Two electrons are in the inner shell and four electrons are in the outer shell. Since elements are most stable when they have eight electrons in their outer shell, carbon needs to either lose four or gain four electrons. This is not easy, so instead, carbon shares its electrons with other elements to form what are called covalent bonds. In this way, carbon will combine with many other elements to form many different compounds.

Carbon is one of the most important elements in all living things. Therefore, carbon compounds are called organic compounds. All plant and animal cells are made from organic compounds. Because carbon is essential to all living things, God has designed a way for carbon to be recycled in what is called the carbon cycle. First, plants absorb carbon in the form of carbon dioxide gas from the air. This carbon dioxide is used in the photosynthesis process to form sugar. Next, animals eat the plants containing sugar and absorb the carbon through digestion. Much of the carbon is released back into the atmosphere through respiration when the animal breathes, exhaling carbon dioxide. Some carbon remains in the animal's body. When an animal dies, its body decays and the carbon enters the soil. Finally, bacteria and fungi in the soil absorb the carbon from the soil, convert it into carbon dioxide, and release it into the air to begin the cycle again.

Drawing the carbon cycle

Draw a picture demonstrating the carbon cycle. Be sure to include plants performing photosynthesis, animals eating plants and exhaling carbon dioxide, and animals and plants decaying. You may also want to include coal being formed in the earth and/or being mined and burned to return carbon to the air. Finally, draw arrows showing which direction the carbon is moving.

Many plants are not eaten by animals, but this does not mean that the carbon in those plants is lost. When a plant dies, it decays and the carbon enters the soil. Again, bacteria and fungi absorb the carbon and release it into the air as carbon dioxide. Also, some plants that have been buried under a large amount of mud or rock and have experienced great pressure have turned into coal. When coal is mined and then burned, it releases carbon dioxide back into the air to be used by plants again. So you can see that God designed a wonderful way to allow carbon atoms to be used over and over again to sustain life on earth. ✳

 # What did we learn?

- What is the atomic number and atomic structure of carbon?
- What makes a compound an organic compound?
- Name two common forms of carbon.
- What is one by-product of burning coal?

 # Taking it further

- How does the carbon cycle demonstrate God's care for His creation?
- What is the most likely event that caused coal formation?
- What would happen if bacteria and fungi did not convert carbon into carbon dioxide gas?

 # Examining carbon

Purpose: To examine a carbon sample

Materials: candle, ceramic plate, knife

Procedure:

1. Hold a ceramic plate about 5 inches above a burning candle.

2. Slowly lower the plate until a black film forms on the bottom of the plate. This film is composed of carbon atoms.

3. Scrape the carbon from the bottom of the plate and feel it.

4. Use the carbon to write/smear a message on a piece of paper.

Questions:

- How does the carbon look? How does the carbon feel?
- Do you think these carbon atoms are more like graphite or diamond?

Carbon allotropes

Carbon atoms can link with other carbon atoms in several different ways. When atoms of the same element link together in different ways to form substances with different properties, the different formations are called **allotropes**. For centuries scientists have known about several common allotropes of carbon. The most common form of carbon is coal. The carbon atoms in coal do not have a specific pattern. Carbon, in the form of diamonds, has a crystalline structure where each carbon atom is linked to four

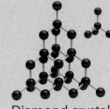

Diamond crystal

other carbon atoms forming a tetrahedron. These tetrahedrons bond with other tetrahedrons to form large crystals. This allotrope of carbon is the strongest naturally occurring substance on earth.

Graphite, on the other hand, is formed when carbon atoms link together to form sheets of hexagons. This is another allotrope of carbon. These sheets stack on top of each other and have weak forces holding the sheets together. This is why graphite molecules easily slip over one another, making graphite a good lubricant. Graphite is also mixed with clay to form pencil lead. The more graphite in the lead, the softer it is.

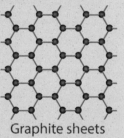

Graphite sheets

In 1985 a new allotrope, or molecular structure, for carbon molecules was discovered by three scientists, Harold W. Kroto, Robert F. Curl, and Richard E. Smalley. These scientists were studying the composition of carbon-rich stars. In their experiments they discovered a new form of carbon that always consisted of 60 atoms. After further experimentation, they found that these molecules were shaped like spheres with the atoms connecting together with hexagons and pentagons just like a soccer ball. They named these balls after the famous architect Buckminster Fuller who developed the geodesic dome. They are called **buckminsterfullerene** or **buckyballs** for short. The discovery of this form of carbon has opened up a whole new field of chemistry. In 1996 Harold Kroto, Richard Smalley, and Robert

Curl shared the Nobel Prize in Chemistry for their discovery of buckminsterfullerene.

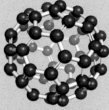

Buckyball

Several other related allotropes have been discovered in recent years. Graphene is similar to graphite as it forms a sheet of hexagons. However, graphene is only one atom thick; it only has one sheet of atoms instead of many sheets. Graphene has unusual electrical properties, and studies are being conducted to see if it can be used to replace semiconductors in many applications.

One of the newest fields of chemistry is called **nanotechnology**, which is the manipulation of matter on the atomic or molecular level for technological uses. Carbon atoms are being used to form structures called nanotubes. **Carbon nanotubes** are formed when a sheet of graphite or a sheet of graphene is formed into a cylinder, usually with a half of a buckyball at one end. These cylinders have special properties that make them very useful. First they are extremely strong. Carbon nanotubes can be 100 times stronger than reinforced steel. There are obvious uses for very strong fibers. For example, the bicycle ridden by Floyd Landis in the 2006 Tour de France used carbon nanotubes to reinforce the carbon frame, making it very strong but extremely light.

A second important property of nanotubes is their ability to conduct electricity. Depending on how they are made, some nanotubes conduct electricity better than silver or copper. Other nanotubes are semiconductors. Although they are not yet being used in production, it is believed that nanotechnology has the potential to replace much of the semiconductor technology being used today.

A third property of nanotubes is their ability to slide inside each other with nearly no friction. Scientists have been able to make tiny motors and rotors that are almost frictionless. This has great potential for tiny machines in the future. Although nanotechnology is very new, it has great potential in many areas. Keep your eyes and ears open to the news, and you will likely hear more about nanotechnology in the future.

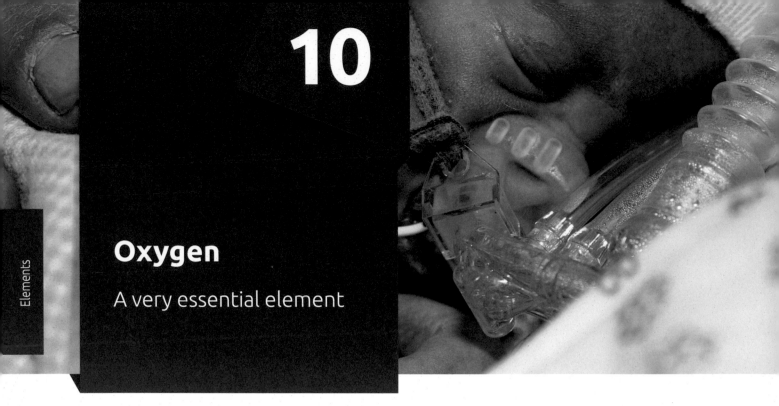

10

Oxygen

A very essential element

What is special about oxygen?

Words to know:

oxidation

The most abundant element on earth is oxygen. Oxygen is also believed to be the fourth most abundant element in the universe. Oxygen is element number 8 on the periodic table of the elements. It has 8 protons and usually has 8 neutrons in its nucleus. Oxygen is in column VIA because it has six valence electrons. This means that oxygen needs two electrons added to its outer shell to be stable.

Most often oxygen atoms are found in the atmosphere as O_2, where two oxygen atoms have bonded together to form what is called a diatomic molecule. These two atoms share electrons so they are said to have covalent bonds. A small percentage of oxygen atoms combine in groups of three atoms, O_3, also known as ozone. Most of the ozone is high in the atmosphere and protects the earth from harmful radiation coming from the sun. The fact that oxygen near the surface of the earth is O_2 and not O_3 shows God's provision for life; the type of oxygen necessary for breathing is near the surface where people and animals are, and the type of oxygen that would be poisonous is high in the atmosphere where it can help shield the earth without harming us.

Oxygen is also abundant on earth in the form of water. Every water molecule has an oxygen atom in it. So between water and air, oxygen is perhaps the most critical element for life. Oxygen is also found combined with many other elements to form oxides, which are generally rocks. For example, oxygen combines with silicon to form silicon oxide, which is better known as quartz. Adding oxygen to a molecule is called **oxidation**.

Another vital function of oxygen is in the releasing of energy. Oxygen is necessary for most burning

Ozone is a triatomic molecule, consisting of three oxygen atoms.

processes. This may not seem very vital for life; however, just as oxygen is necessary to keep a wood fire burning, oxygen is also necessary to "burn" the food you eat. Oxygen is a key element in the process of converting food into energy. This is why animals need to continually breathe oxygen.

Earth is the only planet in our solar system with an abundant supply of oxygen both in the atmosphere and in the form of water. God designed our planet to be the perfect place for life to exist. ✳

What did we learn?

- What is the atomic structure of oxygen?
- How is ozone different from the oxygen we breathe?

Taking it further

- Why does the existence of ozone in the upper atmosphere show God's provision for life on earth?
- How do animals in the ocean get the needed oxygen to "burn" the food they eat?
- Why are oxygen atoms nearly always combined with other atoms?

Oxygen—needed for burning

Oxygen is a necessary element in the combustion process. Whether you are burning wood for a campfire, a candle for a birthday cake, or the food you eat for energy, oxygen is necessary.

Purpose: To demonstrate the necessity for oxygen in combustion

Materials: small candle, glass cup, gloves, dry ice

Activity 1—Procedure:

1. Light a small candle.
2. Cover the candle completely with a glass cup. After a few seconds the candle will go out. Why?

Conclusion: The flame has used up the oxygen in the air and if no new air can reach the flame the burning will stop.

Activity 2—Procedure:

1. Using gloves, place a small piece of dry ice in an open container.
2. Remove the glass and relight the candle from the first activity.
3. Scoop a cup of gas from the container with the dry ice in it and pour the gas above the lighted candle. What happened to the candle? It went out.

Conclusion: Dry ice is frozen carbon dioxide so the gas in the container is carbon dioxide gas. Carbon dioxide gas is heavier than air so when you pour it over the candle it pushes the air molecules out of the way; it moves the oxygen away from the flame and the flame dies. So you can see that oxygen in the air is a very important element.

Oxidation

You have just demonstrated that oxygen is needed for burning, which is rapid oxidation. However, oxygen is also needed for slow oxidation processes. Cellular respiration is the "burning" of food for energy. This is a slow oxidation process. In cellular respiration a glucose molecule is combined with six oxygen molecules (O_2) to form six carbon dioxide molecules and six water molecules. The chemical equation for this process is:

$$C_6H_{12}O_6 + 6\,O_2 \longrightarrow 6\,CO_2 + 6\,H_2O + Energy$$

All animal and plant cells must perform cellular respiration to obtain the necessary energy for growth and activity. Oxygen must be present for this to take place.

You also learned that oxygen combines with many other elements in the earth's crust. This often produces useful compounds. However, sometimes this chemical reaction can cause problems. One oxidation reaction that is not helpful is rusting. Oxygen slowly combines with iron to produce iron oxide, which we commonly call rust. Iron is strong, but rust is brittle and easily breaks down. We often coat things made from iron with paint or other coatings to keep the oxygen away from the iron. This helps to slow down the rusting process.

Water is an important part of the rusting process. Although rust is the combination of oxygen and iron, this is a very slow reaction. Water is a catalyst, which is a substance that speeds up a reaction but is not used up in the process. So rust occurs in areas with high humidity more than in areas of low humidity. Also, salts and other substances in the water can also speed up the rusting process.

Purpose: To observe the use of oxygen in the rusting process

Materials: steel wool, water, dish soap, two test tubes, pencil, dish

Procedure:

1. Cut two strips of steel wool, approximately the same size.

2. Wash one strip with dish soap to remove any oil on the steel wool. Rinse away all the soap, but leave the steel wool moist. Keep the other strip dry.

3. Place each strip in a test tube. Use a pencil to gently push the steel wool to the bottom of the test tubes.

4. Place 1–2 inches of water in a small dish and place the dish in a location where it will not be disturbed.

5. Turn the test tubes upside down and place them in the water.

6. After 12–24 hours, check the level of the water in each tube.

Questions:

- What do you observe?

- Which sample of wool has the most rust?

- Is the water higher in one tube than in the other tube? Why?

Conclusion: The moistened steel wool had the water needed to speed up the reaction so the iron in this tube was able to quickly react with the oxygen in the air to produce more rust than in the test tube without water. As the oxygen in the tube is used up it creates a vacuum in the tube. This draws water into the tube. The air is approximately 21% oxygen. If all of the oxygen in the tube has been used up, the water should fill approximately ⅕ of the tube. You should observe that the water level in the tube with the moistened steel wool is much higher than the water level in the tube with the dry steel wool.

UNIT 3

Bonding

◊ **Describe** the differences between ionic and covalent bonds.

◊ **Demonstrate** different bonds using models.

◊ **Describe** the properties of crystals.

11

Ionic Bonding

Giving up electrons

How do atoms bond together?

Words to know:

chemical formula	ion
electronegativity	ionic bond
low electronegativity	ionic compound
high electronegativity	

Challenge words:

cation	valence
anion	

In general atoms do not exist long as single atoms. Most of them bond with other atoms to form molecules. Some molecules are small and consist of only two atoms. Others are large and can contain hundreds of atoms. To easily describe which atoms make up a particular molecule scientists write out its chemical formula. A **chemical formula** contains the symbol for each type of atom in the molecule followed by a subscripted number showing how many of that type of atom are in the molecule. If there is only one of a particular atom in the molecule there is no number after the symbol. You are probably familiar with the chemical formula

for water, H_2O. This formula shows us that a water molecule consists of two hydrogen atoms and one oxygen atom. The chemical formula for methane is CH_4, one carbon and four hydrogen atoms. This is a quick and easy way to describe a molecule.

Linus Pauling established the concept of electronegativity in 1932.

Atoms chemically connect with other atoms based on the number of valence electrons each atom has. Remember that valence electrons are the electrons in the outermost energy level of the atom. Scientists have determined that each atom is most stable when its outermost level is filled with eight electrons. The only exceptions to this are hydrogen and helium, which only have two electrons in their outermost level.

The ability of an atom to attract electrons to itself is called **electronegativity**. Electronegativity increases as you go from left to right on the periodic table. Atoms with one or two valence electrons easily give up those electrons when they bond with other atoms, allowing the next level in to become the outermost level, so that their outermost level will be full. For example, sodium has one valence electron in the third energy level. If a sodium atom gives up that electron, the second level is now the outermost level with electrons. The second level already has eight electrons so the sodium atom is now stable. Atoms that do not strongly attract electrons from other atoms are said to have a **low electronegativity** and easily give up their valence electrons. Sodium has low electronegativity and easily gives up its one valence electron.

Atoms with six or seven valence electrons easily pull electrons away from other atoms when they bond. These atoms are said to have **high electronegativity**; they hold tightly to their electrons. Chlorine has seven valence electrons. It has high electronegativity and strongly attracts electrons to itself while holding on tightly to its own valence electrons.

When an atom gains or loses electrons, it becomes electrically charged and is called an **ion**. When electrons are transferred as atoms bond, the bond that is formed is called an **ionic bond**. One of the most common substances that is formed by ionic bonding is table salt—sodium chloride (NaCl). Sodium is in the alkali metal family and has one valence electron. Chlorine is in the halogen family and has seven valence electrons. In order to be stable, sodium must lose its one valence electron

Atomic models

Purpose: To make models of a lithium atom and a fluorine atom, and to use those models to demonstrate ionic bonding

Materials: colored mini-marshmallows, toothpicks, glue

Procedure:

1. To make each model, use different colored mini-marshmallows for each part of the atom. If you have these colors, use green marshmallows to represent protons, yellow to represent neutrons, and orange to represent electrons.

2. Lithium has three protons and four neutrons in its nucleus. So glue together three green and four yellow marshmallows.

3. After these have dried, break a toothpick in half and put an electron (orange marshmallow) on the end of each half. Insert these toothpicks into the nucleus.

4. Place an electron on the end of an unbroken toothpick and insert it in the nucleus as well. This is a model of a lithium atom. Notice how two of the electrons orbit closely to the nucleus and one electron is farther away, in the outer shell.

5. Repeat the process to make a fluorine atom. Fluorine has 9 protons and 10 neutrons in its nucleus, so glue together 9 green and 10 yellow marshmallows. The marshmallows for the nucleus can be stacked together to form a ball.

6. After the glue has dried, again break a toothpick in half and use these short pieces to add two electrons to the atom.

7. Finally, add 7 full-length toothpicks with electrons to the nucleus. You now have an atom that has 9 electrons, with 7 of those electrons in the outer shell.

8. Now demonstrate how a lithium atom and a fluorine atom would combine by removing the valence electron from the lithium atom and adding it to the fluorine atom. Now the lithium atom has a positive charge, since it lost an electron, and the fluorine atom has a negative charge, since it gained an electron. These atoms will be attracted to each other and form an ionic bond.

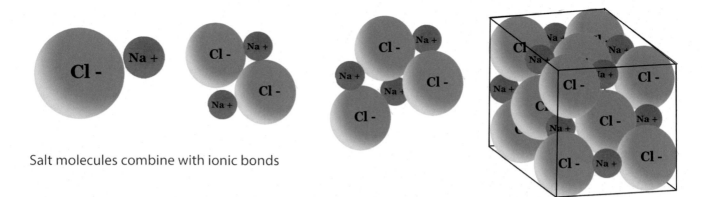

Salt molecules combine with ionic bonds

and chlorine must gain one electron. When sodium and chlorine atoms combine, the chlorine pulls one electron away from the sodium.

The chlorine atom now has one more electron than protons so it has a negative charge. It is now a negative ion. The sodium atom now has one less electron than protons so it is a positively charged ion. These two atoms stay bonded together by their opposite charges and now form the compound sodium chloride. Salt crystals are formed when the positively charged sodium side of a salt molecule lines up with the negatively charged chlorine side of another salt molecule. These opposite charges hold the molecules together. Salt molecules line up to form crystal lattices as shown in the diagram above.

All **ionic compounds**, those formed by exchanging electrons, have similar characteristics. First, ionic compounds are formed from elements that have very different electronegativities. One element always has a high electronegativity, the other has a low electronegativity. Ionic compounds are also brittle and have high melting points. Because they are only held together by their opposite charges, ionic compounds are easily dissolved in water. The oxygen side of a water molecule is slightly negative and the hydrogen side is slightly positive; therefore, water easily pulls ionic molecules away from each other, allowing them to dissolve. Ionic compounds also conduct electricity easily when they are melted or dissolved in water. ✳

What did we learn?

- What is the main feature in an atom that determines how it will bond with other atoms?

- What kind of bond is formed when one atom gives up electrons and the other atom takes the electrons from it?

- What is electronegativity?

- Why are compounds that are formed when one element takes electrons from another called ionic compounds?

- What are some common characteristics of ionic compounds?

- Which element has a higher electronegativity, chlorine or potassium?

🚀 Taking it further

- Which column of elements are the atoms in column IA most likely to form ionic bonds with?

- Use the periodic table of the elements to determine the number of electrons that barium would give up in an ionic bond.

Bonding

🏅 Ions

As you just learned, ionic bonding occurs when two ions are attracted to each other. Ions are formed when an atom either loses or gains electrons. If an atom loses one or more electrons it becomes positively charged. A positively charged ion is called a **cation** (KAT-ī-on). In table salt the sodium loses an electron so it is the cation.

An ion that is formed by gaining electrons is called an **anion** (AN-ī-on). Because an anion has more electrons than protons it has a negative charge. The chlorine atom in salt gains an electron so it is the anion in the compound.

The charge of an ion is shown by a superscript + or -. For example, since sodium in table salt has a positive charge, it is shown as Na^+. Similarly, the chlorine in salt is shown as Cl^-. If an ion has gained or lost more than one electron, the magnitude of the charge is shown as well. If calcium were to bond with sulfur, the calcium would lose two electrons and the sulfur would gain two electrons. They would then be designated as Ca^{2+} and S^{2-}.

The number of electrons that an atom is willing to give up or gain is determined by the number of valence electrons in that atom. Thus, the number of electrons an element is willing to give up or accept when forming a compound is called its **valence**. Sodium and chlorine both have a valence of 1 and calcium and sulfur both have a valence of 2. Atoms will form ionic bonds with other atoms that have the same valence, but very different electronegativities.

Look at the periodic table of the elements. Which types of elements have low electronegativities? If you said metals, or alkali and alkali-earth metals, you are correct. Which kinds of elements have high electronegativities?

Table salt is an Ionic compound of sodium cations and chloride anions.

Nonmetals have high electronegativities. Thus, ionic compounds are only formed between metals and nonmetals.

In order to help people remember when a substance is an ionic compound, scientists change the ending of the name of the nonmetal. You have probably heard salt called sodium chloride. It is an ionic compound formed from sodium and chlorine. To show that it is an ionic compound the ending of chlorine is changed to "ide" and is thus called chloride.

You can practice naming ions by completing the "Name that Ion" worksheet.

Covalent Bonding

Sharing electrons

What is another way that atoms bond together?

Words to know:

covalent bonding

Elements that give up electrons when they bond with other elements form ionic bonds. Ionic bonds occur between elements with very different numbers of valence electrons, however not all compounds are formed by ionic bonding. Sometimes atoms have a similar number of valence electrons and do not easily give them up. In this case, the elements share electrons when they bond. This type of bonding is called **covalent bonding**.

Compounds made by covalent bonding have very different characteristics from those formed by ionic bonding. Covalent compounds have low melting points. They are usually strong and flexible. They are also lightweight, and many do not easily dissolve in water. Because covalent compounds do not form ions, they do not conduct electricity very well. Also, because covalent compounds do not form ions, these molecules have only a slight attraction for each other compared to ionic compounds.

One common type of compound formed by covalent bonding is a diatomic molecule. For example, oxygen gas almost always occurs as O_2— two oxygen atoms bonded together. Each atom of oxygen has 6 valence electrons. None of these atoms will easily give up its electrons. However, when two oxygen atoms bond, they each share two of the other atom's electrons, thus making each atom seem to have a full 8 electrons in its outer shell. This allows the O_2 molecule to be stable because each atom is stable.

Covalent bonding does not just occur between two identical atoms. Bonds between nonmetals are usually covalent. The most common covalent compound on earth is water. Hydrogen has one valence electron and oxygen has six. You might think that the oxygen would pull the electron away from each of the hydrogen atoms to form ionic bonds. However, each hydrogen needs only one additional electron to have a full outer shell so it does not give up its electron as easily as other elements with only one valence electron. Therefore, two hydrogen atoms share their electrons with one oxygen atom and the oxygen shares one of its electrons with each of the hydrogen atoms to form a water molecule. In this way, each atom feels like it has a full outer shell, so the compound is stable.

Scientists have developed a visual way to show the sharing of valence electrons. They write the atomic symbol with dots representing the valence

More atomic models

Purpose: To demonstrate covalent bonding

Materials: colored mini-marshmallows, toothpicks, glue

Procedure:

1. Make marshmallow models for one oxygen and two hydrogen atoms. Use the same color of marshmallows as you did in lesson 11. Hydrogen atoms are extremely easy to make because they have only one proton and one electron. An oxygen atom has 8 protons and 8 neutrons in its nucleus and 8 electrons orbiting the nucleus.

Break a toothpick in half and use the two shorter pieces for the first two electrons, thus showing that the 6 remaining electrons are in the outer shell.

2. Once the models are complete, set the hydrogen atoms close to the oxygen atom in such a way that the electrons of all three atoms form a group of 8 electrons in the outer layer around the nucleus of the oxygen atom. This demonstrates a covalent bond. Do not remove any electrons from any of the atoms.

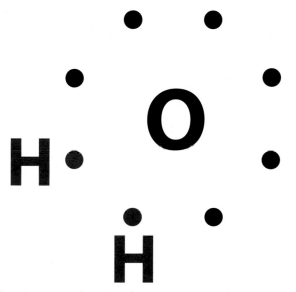

A dot diagram showing how hydrogen and oxygen atoms share electrons

electrons. Above is a dot diagram showing how the hydrogen and oxygen atoms share electrons. The electrons from the hydrogen atoms are shown in a different color from the electrons from the oxygen atom. You can see that the two electrons from the hydrogen atoms give the oxygen atom a full eight electrons and two electrons from the

oxygen atom make the hydrogen atoms feel like they have a full outer shell as well since they need only two valence electrons.

Covalent compounds are vital to life. Not only is water a covalent compound, but most of the compounds that make up our bodies are covalent compounds. These include proteins, fats, and carbohydrates. ✳

What did we learn?

- What is a covalent bond?
- What are some common characteristics of covalent compounds?
- What is the most common covalent compound on earth?

Taking it further

- Why do diatomic molecules form covalent bonds instead of ionic bonds?
- Would you expect more compounds to form ionic bonds or covalent bonds?

🎖 Ionic vs. covalent

Ionic compounds and covalent compounds have very different characteristics. Because ionic compounds are formed from ions, which are electrically charged particles, they readily conduct electricity when they are dissolved in water. However, because covalent compounds are sharing electrons, they do not easily give up electrons so they do not conduct electricity.

You can conduct an experiment to see which substances are ionic compounds and which substances are covalent compounds. Because water is a covalent compound we know that pure water does not conduct electricity. However, the water from your tap is not pure water. There are small amounts of minerals dissolved in tap water. Therefore, you need to use distilled water for this experiment.

Purpose: To determine which compounds are ionic and which are covalent

Materials: "Bonding Experiment" worksheet, four paper cups, distilled water, copper wire, 9-volt battery, baking soda, sugar, salt, olive oil

Procedure:

1. Look at the chemical formula for each of the substances we will be testing. These are listed on the "Bonding Experiment" worksheet. Next to each substance write whether it is composed of all metals, all nonmetals, or both metals and nonmetals. Use a periodic table if you need to see which elements are metals and nonmetals.

2. Based on what the compounds are composed of, make a reasonable guess, called a hypothesis, about whether you think each substance will conduct electricity. Write your guesses on the worksheet. Now you are ready to test your hypotheses.

3. Fill four paper cups with distilled water.

4. Strip off at least 1–2 inches of insulation from each end of 2 copper wires.

5. Attach a length of copper wire to each terminal of a 9 volt battery.

6. Place the ends of the two wires into one of the cups of water. Watch to see if anything happens at the ends of the wires. If electricity is being conducted, you should see small bubbles forming on the ends of the wires. This is because the energy from the moving electrons breaks apart some of the water molecules and the hydrogen gas will collect on one wire and the oxygen gas will collect on the other wire. If you see bubbles, then electricity is being conducted. If you do not see any bubbles, then no electricity is being conducted. Write your observations on your worksheet. After a few seconds, remove the wires from the water.

7. Now, dissolve one teaspoon of baking soda in the first cup, one teaspoon of sugar in the second cup, one teaspoon of salt in the third cup, and one teaspoon of olive oil in the fourth cup. The oil will not really dissolve, but stir it into the water.

8. Use your battery and wire set-up to test for the conduction of electricity in each solution. Be sure to wipe off the wires after each test. Write your observations on your worksheet.

9. Finally, complete the worksheet by writing your conclusions about each compound. Decide if each compound is ionic or covalent.

Metallic Bonding

Sharing on a large scale

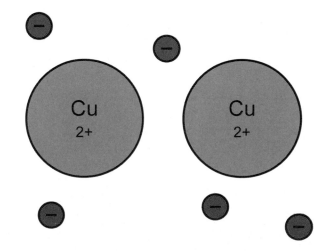

How do metal elements bond together?

Words to know:

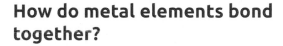

free electron model   metallic bonding

It is easy to see how metals and nonmetals such as sodium and chlorine exchange electrons to form ionic bonds. Sodium gives up one electron so its outermost shell has 8 electrons and chlorine accepts one electron to make 8 electrons in its outermost shell. It is also easy to understand how nonmetals can form covalent bonds by sharing electrons. Two oxygen atoms can share two electrons so that each atom feels that it has 8 electrons in its outer shell. However, it is more difficult to understand how metals can bond with each other. For example, aluminum, with three valence electrons, cannot form ionic bonds with other aluminum atoms. If one aluminum atom gave up its three valence electrons, the other atom would then have six valence electrons and would not be stable. If one atom gave up its three valence electrons to two other atoms there would still not be enough electrons to make the atoms stable. So you can see that metals do not form ionic bonds with other metals.

Similarly, metals do not form covalent bonds. Since metals usually have only one, two, or three valence electrons, two or three atoms together would not have enough electrons to share to make all of the atoms stable. The best explanation for how metals form bonds is called the **free electron model**. This model states that metals share electrons on a grand scale. Thousands of atoms join together and electrons freely move from one atom to another to form stable atoms. This type of bonding is called **metallic bonding**.

Metallic bonds are found in metals like copper, with free electrons among a lattice of positively-charged metal ions.

This free movement of electrons explains why most metals are good conductors of electricity. Compounds formed by metallic bonds also have other similar characteristics. The free movement of electrons allows metals to conduct heat and gives metals their shiny appearance. They also have high melting points and are insoluble in water.

You can see that because elements can form ionic bonds, covalent bonds, and metallic bonds, God has created elements that can produce a nearly endless variety of compounds. This is one reason why our world is so wonderful and so complex. ✳

 What did we learn?

- What is the free electron model?
- How many valence electrons do metals usually have?
- What are common characteristics of metallic compounds?

 Taking it further

- Why don't metals form ionic or covalent bonds?
- Would you expect semiconductors to form metallic bonds?

 Metal models

Purpose: To demonstrate metallic bonding

Materials: colored mini-marshmallows, toothpicks, glue

Procedure:

1. Using marshmallows and toothpicks, make three or more beryllium models. Beryllium has 4 protons and 5 neutrons. It also has 4 electrons, two in its inner shell and two in its outer shell.

2. After making the models, place the models near each other. Note that none of the atoms has enough electrons to be stable.

3. Add some free electrons around the models. These represent the electrons that are shared freely among thousands of metal atoms in metallic bonds. Use the models made in the previous lessons as well as the ones made today to review the differences between ionic, covalent, and metallic bonds.

 Bonding characteristics

Because bonding occurs on an atomic level, you cannot see if a compound is ionic, covalent, or metallic. However, you have learned that each type of compound has certain characteristics. If a substance has the characteristics of an ionic compound it probably has ionic bonds; if it has the characteristics of a metal, it probably has metallic bonds. Review the characteristics listed in the previous lessons, then fill in the "Bonding Characteristics" worksheet.

Mining & Metal Alloys

Making it stronger

How do we process and use metals?

Words to know:

smelting

alloy

electrolysis

Challenge words:

super alloy

Most metals will form metallic bonds with other metal elements, and they form ionic bonds with nonmetals as well. Most metal found in nature is not in a pure metal form. Most commonly, metal atoms combine with oxygen atoms to form metal oxides. To obtain pure metal from the metal ore, a chemical reaction must take place that will remove the oxygen from the metal ore. This type of reaction is called a reduction reaction. The process used to remove oxygen varies depending on the type of metal.

Many metal ores are purified through a process called **smelting**. For example, copper ore is smelted to reduce the amount of oxygen in it. During smelting the ore is crushed and heated. Then hydrogen is blown through the molten metal. The hydrogen combines with the oxygen in the liquid to form water; leaving nearly pure copper behind.

Further refining of copper is done by **electrolysis**. Carbon electrodes are used to pass an electrical current through the liquid copper. This allows any remaining oxygen atoms to combine with carbon atoms from the electrode to form carbon dioxide and allows the pure copper to collect on the other electrode. This results in nearly pure sheets of copper.

A similar process is used to produce pure aluminum. Bauxite is an ore that contains aluminum. The bauxite is dissolved in a cryolite solution (sodium aluminum fluoride), and then placed in an electrolysis set-up like the one shown on the next page. The liquid aluminum collects on the bottom when electricity is passed through the solution, and oxygen combines with the carbon in the electrodes becoming carbon dioxide and escapes from the solution.

Metals like copper and aluminum are very useful because they can be molded into pipes or cans, or drawn into wires. However, pure metals are not always the best choice for a particular job. Scientists have found that by adding a small amount of another element to the molten ore, the resulting metal has superior qualities. When a small amount of one metal is added to another metal the result is called an **alloy**. Alloys are often stronger, more

🧪 Polishing silver

When a metal combines with oxygen, an oxide is produced. Iron oxide is commonly called rust. Copper combines with oxygen to form a layer that is green instead of the shiny reddish-gold we commonly think of as copper. The Statue of Liberty is made of copper, but is green because the copper has oxidized.

Silver also oxidizes. We usually say that silver has tarnished when the silver combines with oxygen. This oxidation leaves a streaky black surface on our silverware and other silver items. Because people prefer silver to be shiny and silvery, scientists have developed tarnish remover. Tarnish remover is usually a liquid or cream that combines chemically with the silver oxide, leaving behind a shiny silvery surface.

Remove silver oxide from a piece of silver that is tarnished. Follow the directions on the tarnish remover. This will allow you to perform a chemical reaction and help restore the beauty of your silver at the same time.

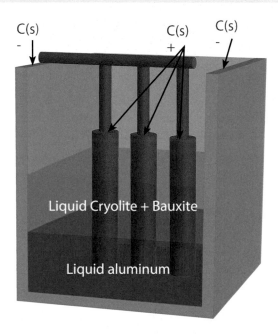

C(s) −   C(s) +   C(s) −

Liquid Cryolite + Bauxite

Liquid aluminum

resilient, and easier to work with than the pure metal would be. For example, steel is iron with a small amount of carbon added. Steel is stronger and more flexible than iron.

To produce steel, iron ore is processed in a blast furnace. First, the ore is crushed. Then it is mixed with limestone and coke (a form of carbon—not the soft drink). This mixture is then heated to very high temperatures in a blast furnace. The resulting molten metal is called pig iron. This is iron with a significant amount of carbon in it. Pig iron can be cast into pots and other shapes, but it is brittle and is not useful for most other applications. To improve the quality of the iron, when the molten iron is removed from the furnace, oxygen is blown through the liquid where it combines with the carbon to form carbon dioxide, which bubbles out of the liquid. The remaining liquid is iron with just a small amount of carbon. This is called steel. Steel is pliable and strong and can be formed into rods, sheets, and other shapes that are useful for many applications.

Other elements besides carbon are sometimes added to steel to further improve its performance. For example, chromium is added to produce stainless steel. This metal does not easily corrode so it is preferable for many applications, such as making forks and spoons to eat with. Another element that is sometimes added to steel is tungsten. Tungsten makes steel very tough. Tungsten steel is often used to make saw blades that last longer than regular steel blades. ✳

Steel can be formed into many useful applications.

What did we learn?

- What element is combined with most metals to form metal ore?

- What must be done to metal oxides to obtain pure metal?

- What is an alloy?

- Why are alloys produced?

 # Taking it further

- Do you think chromium would be added to steel that is going to be used in saw blades? Why or why not?

- Is oxidation of metal always a bad thing?

Alloys

Pure metals are used in some applications. For instance, pure gold is used to cover the dome of the Colorado state capital building. However, in many applications metal alloys are used because they are stronger. But why are alloys stronger than pure metals? When pure metals bond together, they generally form straight lines of atoms. If something disrupts the atoms, they can break apart in sheets or **crack** in straight lines. However, if a small amount of another metal is added to the original metal while it is molten, the new atoms mix into the middle of the original metal atoms. This keeps the atoms from forming into long lines and actually makes the metal stronger.

Some alloys are very strong, even at high temperatures. These metals are called **super alloys**. Super alloys have nickel, iron, and cobalt added to make them strong.

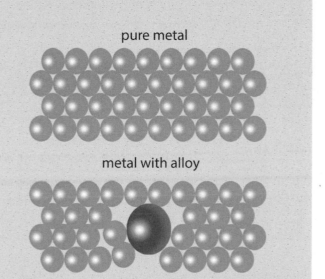

pure metal

metal with alloy

See what you can find out about some common alloys by completing the "Common Alloys" worksheet.

Charles Martin Hall

1863–1914

Aluminum, believed to be the most common metal on earth, was discovered by Friedrich Wohler in 1827. This discovery, however, did not mean that aluminum was immediately available for use. In its natural state, aluminum is always tightly bonded with other compounds; most often it is in a compound called bauxite. Without an economical method for extracting the aluminum from the bauxite, pure aluminum was very expensive. During most of the mid 1800s, aluminum was so valuable that it was mostly used in jewelry and for special projects, like capping the Washington Monument. Because the unique properties of aluminum made it ideal for many applications, a race was on to find a less expensive way to extract it from the ore. Two men, working independently from each other, won this race. These two men, Charles Martin Hall of the U.S. and Paul Heroult of France, were born the same year (1863), made their discoveries the same year (1886) and died the same year (1914).

Charles Martin Hall was born in Thompson, Ohio, to Rev. Heman Hall and Sophronia Brooks Hall. When he was 10 years old, Charles and his family moved to Oberlin, Ohio. There he did his preparatory work in high school and, in 1880, began his studies at Oberlin College.

Charles did not take a formal chemistry class until his junior year in college; however, his interest in chemistry began much earlier. Hall met Dr. Frank Jewett, a well-educated chemist, while buying some equipment and chemicals during his first year of college. Hall and Jewett spent many hours discussing chemistry, and it is believed that Jewett was instrumental in encouraging and helping Hall in his discovery of aluminum extraction. In class, Jewett talked about the challenge of finding an economical

method for extracting aluminum. Jewett said, "Any person who discovers a process by which aluminum can be made on a commercial scale will bless humanity and make a fortune for himself." Charles Hall took the challenge and told some of his fellow students, "I'm going for that metal."

Jewett, along with Charles's sister Julia, made many contributions to the discovery. In addition to working in a lab in the woodshed behind his house, Hall was allowed to use Jewett's personal laboratory. Jewett also supplied Hall with materials and up-to-date knowledge of chemistry. Jewett had gone to one of the best schools in Europe for his education, and before coming to Oberlin College, he taught at the Imperial University of Tokyo, so he was a valuable asset in Hall's quest for aluminum.

Charles's sister Julia had also gone to Oberlin College and had taken most of the same science courses he had taken. She was very involved in his research and probably helped him prepare many of the chemicals that he used. When he finally made his successful experiment on February 9, 1886, he repeated the experiment for Julia the next day, after she returned from a trip to Cleveland.

The famous experiment in 1886 used electrolysis to remove the aluminum from aluminum oxide. Hall accomplished this by dissolving aluminum oxide in a cryolite-aluminum fluoride mixture, and then passing an electrical current through the liquid. The electricity caused aluminum to form and settle on the bottom of the vessel where it could not oxidize with the oxygen in the air.

Charles Hall applied for a patent for his aluminum reduction process in July, 1886, only to find that a Frenchman named Paul Heroult had already applied for a patent for the same process. How could two people in two different parts of the world come up with the same process at virtually the same time? These men were both very interested in solving this problem and had access to much of the same information and the same materials, so it is not surprising that they developed the same process. The patent dispute was resolved when it was confirmed that Hall had performed his successful experiment shortly before Heroult did.

Hall was very successful at overcoming obstacles and within a few years, he and his partners were making commercial quality aluminum. In 1888 he and his partners started the Pittsburgh Reduction Company, and in 1907 the name of the company was changed to the Aluminum Company of America, which is today known as ALCOA.

By 1914 Hall's new process had caused the price of aluminum to drop from $12.00/lb to $0.18/lb. As Jewett had predicted, Hall's discovery truly was a blessing to humanity and made a fortune for him. Today, a host of items are made from aluminum. However, Hall did not keep all of his fortune for himself. He donated over $10 million dollars to Oberlin College. He also donated substantial amounts of money to Berea College, to the American Missionary Association, and to educational programs in Asia and the Balkans.

15

Crystals

Sparkling like diamonds

How are crystals formed?

Words to know:

crystal   edge

face

Challenge words:

hydrated   anhydrous

water of crystallization   dehydration

hydrate

What do salt, sugar, sand, diamonds, and snowflakes all have in common? They are all solids that have a crystalline structure. Certain materials form crystals when the liquid form freezes or becomes a solid. **Crystals** are solids whose atoms are in an orderly pattern. Crystals have flat surfaces called **faces**, and **edges** where their faces meet. There are seven major types or shapes of crystals. These are shown below and on the next page.

Large, perfectly formed crystals can only form when liquids are allowed to cool slowly and are not disturbed. This allows the atoms to line up in the crystal formation. If a liquid cools rapidly, crystals will not form at all, or only very small crystals will form.

The most common place to find crystals is among rocks and minerals. These compounds are the most likely to form crystalline bonds. One very common type of crystal is quartz. Quartz always forms six-sided crystals. Another very interesting place to find crystals is in a geode. A geode is a rock in which crystals have formed in the center. A geode must be broken open to reveal the beauty of the crystals inside.

Some crystals are made of only one kind of element. Diamonds, for example, are pure carbon. But most crystals are made from two or more kinds of atoms.

The seven crystal systems

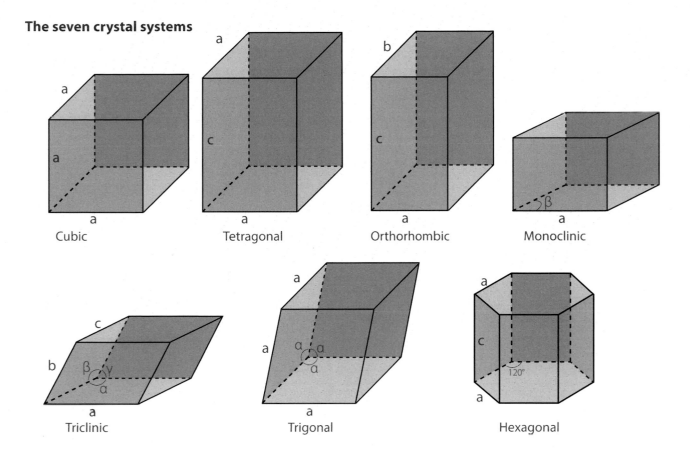

Cubic   Tetragonal   Orthorhombic   Monoclinic

Triclinic   Trigonal   Hexagonal

Other crystals form when minerals which have been dissolved in water crystallize as the water evaporates. Salt crystals often form this way. Crystals that form this way are also common in limestone caves. As water seeps through the limestone, it dissolves small amounts of calcite and gypsum. When the water drips from the ceiling of the cave, it evaporates leaving behind the minerals as stalactites and stalagmites. These crystal formations can be very beautiful.

Not all crystals are formed naturally. The first artificial, or man-made, rubies were made in 1837 by a French scientist named Gaudin. Since that time, the process has been improved and artificial gems are now routinely made. Although some artificial gems, such as cubic zirconia, are crystals that are made to look like real gems but are made from different materials, many artificial gems are crystals made from the same chemicals as the naturally occurring gem. The elements are melted and then allowed to cool very slowly, sometimes under high pressure. Today over 44,000 pounds (20,000 kg) of artificial diamonds are manufactured each year, as well as artificial rubies, sapphires, spinets, and emeralds. Although artificial gems are chemically identical to naturally occurring gems, they are usually not as brilliant as the natural ones.

In addition to gems, crystals have many uses. Some crystals, such as salt and sugar, are part of our

Fun Fact

Salt has been a valuable crystal throughout history. Not only is salt used to season food, it has been used for centuries as a natural preservative. In ancient times, salt was so valuable that it was used as a form of currency. At times, people preferred to be paid in salt rather than gold.

Growing crystals

You can make your own crystals by dissolving minerals in water and then allowing the water to evaporate slowly. This works best when you have a saturated solution. A saturated solution is one that cannot dissolve any more of the material being dissolved. The amount of material that can be dissolved increases with temperature, so you will want to heat the water before dissolving the minerals.

Purpose: To grow two different shapes of crystals

Materials: plate, water, black construction paper, scissors, small pan, stove, table salt, Epsom salt

Procedure:

1. Place a plate upside down on a piece of black or other dark construction paper. Trace around the edge of the plate. Remove the plate and cut out the circle. Place the paper on top of the plate.

2. Place ½ cup of water in a small pan and bring to a boil.

3. Dissolve as much table salt in the water as you can. Add the salt a teaspoon at a time until no more salt will dissolve.

4. Slowly pour the saltwater onto the paper on the plate until the paper is completely wet, but not soaked.

5. Place the plate in a place where it will not be disturbed.

6. Repeat steps 1-5 using Epsom salt instead of table salt

7. Allow the water to evaporate undisturbed for several days. After the water is gone, you should see crystals growing on the paper.

Conclusion: The table salt crystals will be cube-shaped and the Epsom salt crystals will be long needles. When the paper is completely dry, look under the paper. There may be some crystals that formed under the paper as well.

food. Other crystals are used in the medical field as medications, and in hearing aids. Some crystals, like silicon, are used in the semiconductor industry. Diamonds that are not good enough to be gems have many uses because of their hardness. Diamonds are added to drill bits, saw blades, scalpels, and other cutting instruments to make them sharp and hard. There are many other uses for crystals as well. God has blessed us with an abundance of crystals for a variety of purposes. ✳

What did we learn?

*   What is a crystal?
*   How do crystals form?
*   What is an artificial gem?
*   Where would you look to find crystals?

 # Taking it further

*   Why are naturally occurring gems more valuable than artificial gems when many are made from the same materials?

*   Why is a saturated solution better for forming crystals?

*   What are some ways you use crystals in your home?

 # Opening a geode—optional

It is fun to crack open a geode and reveal the crystals inside. If you have access to a geode, open it up and enjoy the beauty hidden inside.

Hydrates

Many salts do not just dissolve in water to form a water solution. Some salts chemically bond with the water. When this occurs the crystals are said to be **hydrated**. The water that is stored in the molecules is called the **water of crystallization** and the substance itself is called a **hydrate**. Although hydrates contain water, they usually do not feel wet because the water molecules are bound to the crystals.

Hydrates have many important uses. One you are probably familiar with is keeping products dry. Have you ever opened a box with a new pair of shoes and found a little packet with crystals inside? The crystals are hydrates that can absorb more water. They are included to prevent your new shoes from getting moist when they are shipped. Other products including purses, wallets, and some food products also contain hydrate packets to absorb excess moisture.

Another important use of hydrates is in the making of fire resistant materials such as housing insulation. The materials used often have hydrates in them. This is important because if there is a fire in your house, the heat will cause the water in the hydrates to evaporate. This will use up energy from the fire, which keeps the fire from spreading. The more hydrates in the material the longer it will resist the spreading of fire.

Heating will usually remove the water from hydrates, leaving behind a dry solid. The dry solid is said to be **anhydrous**. The process of removing water is called **dehydration**. Anhydrous crystals are also used in many applications. You probably have concrete in the foundation of your house. Concrete is formed when cement, which is an anhydrous crystal, is mixed with water. The water causes a chemical reaction as it bonds with the crystals. This releases energy, which is why you might see steam coming off of newly poured cement. However, not all of the water is evaporated; some of it is bonded with the cement and actually gives strength to the concrete.

You can experience your own chemical reaction with an anhydrous crystal. Plaster of Paris is anhydrous calcium sulfate. When water is added to the powder, it hydrates the crystals and starts a chemical reaction. Some of the water evaporates, leaving behind a network of hydrated crystals that forms a solid.

A fun use of plaster of Paris is in casting animal tracks in the wild. Often a scientists or naturalist will pour a small amount of plaster into an animal track and allow it to dry. Then he can take the mold with him to identify at a later time.

Purpose: To make your own plaster track at home

Materials: modeling clay, water, a pet, plaster of Paris

Procedure:

1. Make a cookie-sized disk of modeling clay.

2. Press your cat's or dog's paw into the clay to make a print. Or make up your own track by making indentations in the clay with your fingers or other objects.

3. Mix ¼ cup of plaster of Paris with enough water to make a creamy liquid.

4. Carefully pour the liquid into the indentations.

5. Allow the plaster to dry for several hours.

6. When the plaster is dry, remove the clay and you will have a plaster cast of your animal track made from a hydrated salt.

16

Ceramics

Making it with clay

What are ceramics, and how are they made?

Words to know:

ceramics

Challenge words:

bioceramics

resorbable ceramics

inert ceramics

active ceramics

Crystals are an essential part of our lives. From computers to jewelry, we use crystals every day. One very special type of crystal material is ceramic. **Ceramics** are inorganic nonmetallic materials which are formed by the action of heat. The word *ceramic* comes from the Greek word for *earthenware* and describes where ceramics came from. Traditional ceramics include pottery, brick, porcelain, and glass. And the common ingredient in each of these materials is clay, which comes from the earth, making them earthenware and thus the name, ceramic.

The clay molecules in ceramic materials are fused with other chemicals by heat. The toughness, look, and other characteristics of the ceramic material are determined by the crystal structures that are formed in the heating process. From the ancient Egyptians to the American Indians, people in many cultures have used the heating or firing process to strengthen their earthenware. People have been firing their pottery to make it stronger for thousands of years, long before anyone understood the chemistry behind it. Even at the Tower of Babel, they were baking bricks, more than 4,000 years ago (Genesis 11:3).

Today, with a better understanding of chemical bonding, scientists have developed advanced ceramics. These new ceramics are designed with specific, very pure substances that are fired in very specific ways to create very strong crystal structures. These new ceramics are replacing metal in many applications. The new ceramics are often stronger, harder, and more heat resistant than the metals they

After a clay vessel is made, it is fired to make it strong.

replace. Also, ceramics are more chemically stable. They do not react with oxygen to form rust as readily as metals often do.

New ceramics are engineered for specific purposes. For example, special ceramic material is used to make artificial joints used in medical procedures. This new ceramic material contains calcium that will fuse with the surrounding bone; allowing the new joint to become part of the body. Another special ceramic has been developed for use as heat-absorbing tiles

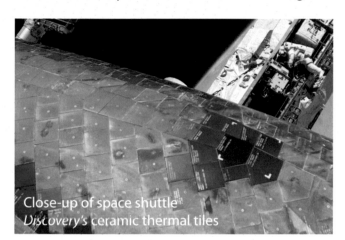

Close-up of space shuttle *Discovery's* ceramic thermal tiles

on the underside of the space shuttle. Ceramics are also being used as tools such as scissors, knives, and blades for machines. As scientists learn more about chemistry, they will be able to continue developing more uses for special ceramics.

What did we learn?

- What is ceramic?
- What are some examples of traditional ceramics?
- What makes ceramics hard?
- What are some advantages of modern ceramics?

Taking it further

- Why are the tiles on the space shuttle made of ceramic?
- Why are crystalline structures stronger than noncrystalline structures?

Fun with clay

One of the most interesting new ceramics to be developed in recent years is polymer clay. Polymer clay is a material that is soft and pliable. It can be molded into any shape and then remolded as often as desired. However, when the clay is baked at a low temperature, a chemical reaction occurs and the clay becomes hard. This clay is fun for children, but has recently become an art medium for adults as well.

Make a sculpture, beads, pots, or other items using polymer clay such as Sculpey or Femo. Follow the manufacturer's directions for baking the finished masterpiece.

⊚ Bioceramics

Ceramics that are used in the human body are called **bioceramics**. We already mentioned a little about how ceramics can be used inside the body, but this is such an interesting topic we knew you would want to learn more about it. There are basically three different kinds of bioceramics: those that do not react at all with the body, those that break down inside the body, and those that combine with the tissues to become a part of the body.

Ceramics that do not react chemically inside the body are called **inert ceramics**. Alumina and zirconia are the most common inert ceramics used in the body. These materials are very hard and can be highly polished for low friction. This makes them ideal for joint replacements for hips and knees. Inert ceramics are sometimes used as spacers in bones where a small section of bone must be removed. The spacer is put in its place as a frame for new bone cells to grow on.

Another inert ceramic is pyrolytic carbon. This ceramic material is often used to replace valves inside a heart. The valves are very strong and can withstand the wear and tear of constant use. Even more importantly, they do not cause blood clots.

Ceramics that break down or dissolve inside the body are called **resorbable ceramics**. These ceramics can be used to deliver drugs, particularly radioactive particles, to a certain location in the body or to provide temporary strength to a bone while the body repairs itself. Most resorbable ceramics are made from calcium phosphates or from silca-based glass ceramics.

Finally, ceramics that react with the body but do not break down are called **active ceramics**. Active materials are often used to coat metal implants. Active ceramics are usually too brittle to be used as a load-bearing structure so titanium or stainless steel is used to replace leg bones or other structures, then the implant is coated with hydroxyapatite, which is an active ceramic.

Hydroxyapatite is made from a material that is chemically very similar to the bones in your spine. This material reacts chemically with the bone material in the patient's body to promote bone growth and to prevent infection in the area. It also helps to prevent rejection of the implant.

The use of bioceramics has helped millions of people to live better lives. This is a growing field of science and new ceramic techniques and devices are being designed every year.

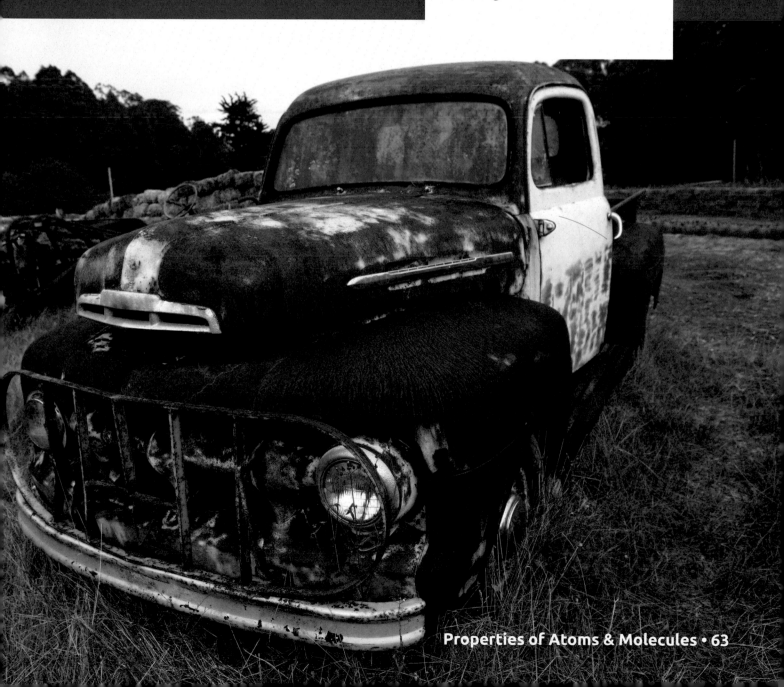

UNIT 4

Chemical Reactions

◊ **Use** equations to describe chemical reactions.

◊ **Identify** factors that effect chemical reactions.

◊ **Demonstrate** the first law of thermodynamics using chemical reactions.

◊ **Describe** what happens to heat during chemical reactions.

Chemical Reactions

Changing from one thing to another

How do chemicals react with each other?

Words to know:

reactants

products

chemical reaction

first law of
    thermodynamics

composition reaction

decomposition reaction

reaction rate

As you learned in the past several lessons, elements bond in many different ways depending on their electron structures. When two or more different elements bond together, a chemical reaction takes place and a new substance is formed. In a chemical reaction, the beginning materials are called the **reactants** and the ending materials are called the **products**. Some common chemical reactions you are probably familiar with include photosynthesis, bread dough rising, a flame burning, or a firecracker exploding.

The formation of water is a very simple chemical reaction. Two hydrogen atoms bond with one oxygen atom to form a water molecule. Hydrogen and oxygen are the reactants and water is the product. Breaking water apart is also a chemical reaction. One water molecule can be broken apart to form two hydrogen atoms and one oxygen atom. In this reaction water is the reactant and hydrogen and oxygen are the products. A **chemical reaction** takes place whenever atomic bonds are formed or broken.

Simple chemical reactions occur when atoms combine to form molecules. But more complex chemical reactions take place when two or more molecules break apart and their atoms recombine to form new molecules. Let's look at a very important chemical reaction taking place all the time—photosynthesis. During photosynthesis molecules of carbon dioxide and water are broken apart and then combined inside a plant's leaf to form molecules of glucose (sugar) and oxygen. This diagram shows how this happens.

$$C_6H_{12}O_6 + 6\,O_2$$
Glucose   Oxygen

$$6\,CO_2 + 6\,H_2O + 54\ \text{photons}$$
Carbon dioxide   Water   light energy

The chemical reaction of photosynthesis

Inside a leaf, six carbon dioxide molecules and six water molecules (the reactants) are broken apart into carbon, hydrogen, and oxygen atoms. Then these atoms combine together to form one molecule of glucose, which uses all of the carbon atoms, all of the hydrogen atoms, and some of the oxygen atoms. The rest of the oxygen atoms combine to form oxygen gas. Glucose and oxygen gas are the products.

It is important to realize that when a chemical reaction takes place the atoms that are in the products are the same atoms that were in the reactants. Just because one substance went away and a new substance was formed does not mean that the original atoms disappeared and new atoms appeared. Once scientists began to understand chemical reactions they realized that there is no way to make new matter, only many ways to rearrange existing matter. This concept is the **first law of thermodynamics**, which says that matter and energy cannot be created or destroyed; they can only change forms. God is the only one who can create new matter or new energy.

Sometimes chemical reactions are reversible. If water is broken apart into oxygen and hydrogen gas, the gases can later be recombined to form water again. Other chemical reactions cannot be reversed. For example, if you cook an egg, the egg cannot be "uncooked." Some chemical reactions happen very easily. You notice an immediate reaction when you combine baking soda and vinegar. Other reactions are slow or may even require heat, light, or other stimuli to make them happen. For example, photosynthesis does not occur without sunlight and chlorophyll.

There are many different kinds of chemical reactions. If an element combines with oxygen, the reaction is called an oxidation reaction. If oxygen is removed from a substance, such as in the purification of metals, the reaction is called a reduction reaction. If elements other than oxygen combine to form a new substance, the reaction is a **composition reaction**, and if a substance is broken down into individual elements, the reaction is a **decomposition reaction**.

Some reactions happen very quickly. In fact, some are instantaneous, like the explosion of fireworks. Other reactions happen very slowly. The rate at which a reaction takes place is called its **reaction rate**. A piece of iron will eventually rust away, but depending on how much iron you start with, it

Fire extinguisher in a jar

A flame is a chemical reaction that requires oxygen. Therefore, it is an oxidation reaction. If you are trying to build a campfire, you need to make sure that air, which contains oxygen, can reach the wood, paper, and other materials you may be using to build your fire. However, if a fire starts someplace you don't want a fire, one of the quickest ways to put out the fire is to deprive it of oxygen; the fire will then go out quickly. This is the way that many fire extinguishers work. The fire extinguisher sprays a chemical on the fire that keeps the oxygen away from the flames and allows the flames to go out.

Purpose: To build a fire extinguisher in a jar

Materials: modeling clay, birthday candle, jar, vinegar, baking soda

Procedure:

1. Using a piece of modeling clay, attach a birthday candle to the inside bottom of a jar.

2. Pour ¼ cup of vinegar into the jar. Be sure not to get the wick of the candle wet.

3. Light the candle.

4. Sprinkle a teaspoon of baking soda into the jar. Be sure not to sprinkle it on the candle.

Conclusion: The candle will quickly go out, even though none of the ingredients you added touched it. The carbon dioxide produced by the reaction of vinegar and baking soda pushes the air out of the jar and deprives the flame of oxygen.

may take years or even decades for the metal to all turn to rust. In order for a chemical reaction to take place, the reactants must be in contact with each other. So the speed of the reaction is not only affected by what kind of reaction is taking place, but also by the size and shape of the reactants. A cube of iron will rust much more slowly than a thin sheet of iron containing the same amount of material because the thin sheet has more surface area and the oxygen in the air can react with more of the iron molecules at one time.

Increasing the concentration of reactants will usually speed up the reaction. The more molecules of each type of reactant there are, the more likely they are to come in contact with each other and react together. So adding more reactants or pushing them closer together will speed up the rate of the reaction.

In other reactions, heat can speed up the rate at which the reaction takes place. Heat causes the molecules to move more quickly so the reactants come in contact with each other more often and the reaction speeds up. Another way to increase the reaction rate of some chemical reactions is to add a catalyst. A catalyst is a substance that is added that encourages the reaction to occur, but is not used up in the reaction. We will explore catalysts more in a later lesson.

It is important to remember that chemical reactions are taking place all around us and even inside us all the time. These reactions are necessary for life and are designed by God to happen in a very predictable way. So enjoy learning about chemical reactions. ✳

What did we learn?

- What is a chemical reaction?
- What are the initial ingredients in a chemical reaction called?
- What are the resulting substances of a chemical reaction called?

Taking it further

- How might you speed up a chemical reaction?
- A fire hose usually sprays water on a fire to put it out. Water does not deprive the fire of oxygen, so why does water put out a fire?
- What chemical reaction do you think is taking place in the making of a loaf of bread?

Temperature & surface area

You just learned that reaction rate can be increased in several ways. What are some of those ways? Two of the most important things that affect reaction rate are temperature and the surface area of the reactants. Here is a fun way to see the effects of temperature and surface area on reaction rate. On a copy of the "Reaction Rate Experiment" worksheet, complete the hypotheses section before conducting the experiments below.

Activity 1

Purpose: To test the effects of temperature on reaction rate

Materials: water, stove, pan, three clear cups, ice, Alka-Seltzer tablets, stop watch, "Reaction Rate Experiment" worksheet

Procedure:

1. Heat a small amount of water until it is boiling.

2. Carefully pour the hot water into a clear cup.

3. Fill a second clear cup with the same amount of room temperature water.

4. Fill a third cup to the same level with a combination of ice and water.

5. Drop an Alka-seltzer tablet into each cup at the same time and start your stop watch.

6. Time how long it takes for each tablet to completely dissolve.

Questions:

- What differences do you observe in each cup?

- Are there more bubbles in one cup than in another?

- Are there fewer bubbles in one cup?

- Which tablet dissolved the fastest?

- Which dissolved the slowest?

- Write your observations on the worksheet.

Activity 2

Purpose: To test the effects of surface area on reaction rate

Materials: water, three clear cups, Alka-Seltzer tablets, paper, spoon, stop watch

Procedure:

1. Fill three clear cups with the same amount of room temperature water.

2. Break an Alka-seltzer tablet into several smaller pieces. Place all of the pieces together on a small sheet of paper.

3. Crush another tablet with the back of a spoon. Be sure to place all of the powder on another small sheet of paper.

4. Place a whole tablet in one cup, all of the pieces of the broken tablet in a second cup, and all of the powder of the crushed tablet in a third cup.

5. Begin your stop watch and again time how long it takes for each tablet to completely dissolve.

Questions:

- Which tablet dissolved first? Which tablet dissolved the slowest? Again, record your observations on the worksheet.

- Did your observations match your hypotheses? If not, try to figure out why you got an unexpected result.

Chemical Reactions

18

Chemical Equations

Describing how it works

How do we write a chemical equation?

Words to know:

chemical equation

Challenge words:

single-displacement reaction

double-displacement reaction

Chemical reactions are taking place all around us, but it may be difficult to understand or visualize what is happening in a reaction. Therefore, scientists have developed a method for describing what is happening in a chemical reaction. This method is called a **chemical equation**.

We could draw pictures of the atoms and molecules to help explain what is going on in a chemical reaction. This would certainly help us visualize what is going on. For example, it is easy to see what is happening in the reaction below. We see that two copper oxide molecules are combined with one carbon atom. The result is two copper atoms bonded together and one molecule of carbon dioxide. While pictures do help us to see what is going on, it quickly becomes difficult to draw pictures of all of the molecules that we know of. Do you remember what a simple sugar molecule (glucose) looks like? It has 6 carbon atoms, 12 hydrogen atoms, and 6 oxygen atoms. This is time consuming to draw and it is still a very small molecule. Some molecules have hundreds of atoms in them.

Because drawing reactions is sometimes difficult, scientists have created an easier way to describe what is going on in a reaction. They use a chemical equation.

Chemical equations work just like mathematical equations. When two quantities are added together in math, you can show that using an equation, such as 4 + 3 = 7. This equation tells you that if you add

This reaction would be written as:

$$2CuO + C \longrightarrow 2Cu + CO_2$$

four apples to three apples you will end up with 7 apples. Similarly, a chemical equation tells you how different elements or compounds combine together to form new compounds. Chemical equations use a plus sign (+) to indicate which compounds are combined or added together, but instead of an equals sign, chemical equations use an arrow to show what the result is. The chemical symbol from the periodic table is used to represent each of the elements being combined. For example, below is the chemical equation for producing water:

$$2H_2 + O_2 \longrightarrow 2H_2O$$

Let's see how we got this equation. We know that water is made from hydrogen and oxygen. So we begin by writing the atomic symbols for hydrogen (H) and oxygen (O) on the left side of the equation with a plus sign between them.

$$H + O$$

This shows what types of atoms are being combined. Next, we draw an arrow to show that a reaction is taking place. Then we write the result on the right side of the arrow. You know that water is H_2O. This means that there are two atoms of hydrogen and one atom of oxygen in a molecule of water.

$$H + O \longrightarrow H_2O$$

There are a couple of problems with this equation. First, as you learned earlier, hydrogen and oxygen seldom occur as single atoms. They commonly occur as diatomic molecules. So let's rewrite the equation to reflect this.

$$H_2 + O_2 \longrightarrow H_2O$$

Finally, we have to make sure there are the same number of atoms on each side of the arrow. How many atoms are shown on the left side of the arrow?

🧪 Chemical equations

Complete the "Understanding Chemical Equations" worksheet.

Four. How many atoms are shown on the right side of the arrow? Three. We have a problem with our equation; it is not complete yet. We need to show that we need two hydrogen diatomic molecules to react with every oxygen diatomic molecule and that when these molecules react they produce two molecules of water. So the complete equation would look like:

$$2H_2 + O_2 \longrightarrow 2H_2O$$

We now have four hydrogen atoms and two oxygen atoms on each side of the equation.

As we learned in the last lesson, the elements or compounds that are added together are called reactants, and the resulting compound is called the product of the reaction. In this case, the hydrogen and oxygen are the reactants and water is the product. This type of reaction, where two or more reactants are combined to form a single product is called a *composition reaction*. It has the general form of:

$$A + B \longrightarrow AB$$

Not all chemical reactions are composition reactions, however. Many reactions are just the opposite. If an electrical current is sent through a sample of water, some of the water molecules will break apart into separate hydrogen and oxygen gas molecules. This type of reaction is called a *decomposition reaction*. The general form of a decomposition equation is:

$$AB \longrightarrow A + B$$

Notice that this format is the opposite of the composition reaction. The compound on the left is still called the reactant, but in this type of reaction there are two or more products. In the water example, water is the reactant and hydrogen and oxygen gas are the products. The equation for the decomposition of water is:

$$2H_2O \longrightarrow 2H_2 + O_2$$

We will learn more about chemical reactions and chemical equations in the upcoming lessons. ✳

What did we learn?

- What is a chemical equation?
- What are the elements or compounds on the left side of a chemical equation called?
- What are the elements or compounds on the right side of a chemical equation called?

Taking it further

- Why is it helpful to use chemical equations?

🏅 Reactants and products

So far we have looked at chemical equations for composition and decomposition reactions. Chemical equations can help us understand other types of chemical reactions as well. Sometimes a compound will combine with an element to form a new compound and a different element. This is shown by the chemical equation:

$$AB + C \longrightarrow AC + B$$

In this reaction, compound AB was broken apart. Then A combined with C leaving B by itself. This type of reaction is called a **single displacement reaction** or a single replacement reaction. Element B was displaced by element C in the chemical bonding. The chemical equation helps us to visualize this reaction. All metal with acid reactions are single displacement reactions. For example, when magnesium combines with hydrochloric acid the magnesium displaces the hydrogen as shown below:

$$Mg + 2HCl \longrightarrow MgCl_2 + H_2$$

Another type of chemical reaction is called a **double displacement reaction** or double replacement reaction. This is demonstrated by the equation:

$$AB + CD \longrightarrow AC + BD$$

In this type of reaction, elements B and C trade places, forming two new compounds. In the equation below you can see that iron (Fe) and hydrogen trade places.

$$Fe_2O_3 + 6HCl \longrightarrow 2FeCl_3 + 3H_2O$$

It is important to note that whatever elements you start with must also end up on the other side of the equation. For a mathematical equation to be true, both sides must be equal. For example, if you place 4 apples in a bowl then add 3 more apples to the bowl, you will have the same number of apples as in a bowl with 7 apples; you will not have 6 or 8 apples. Similarly, for a chemical equation to be true, the number of atoms of each type of element must be the same on each side of the arrow. In the water equation, there were four hydrogen atoms and two oxygen atoms on each side of the equation. Below is the chemical equation for photosynthesis:

$$6CO_2 + 6H_2O \longrightarrow C_6H_{12}O_6 + 6O_2$$

The 6 in front of the CO_2 indicates that 6 carbon dioxide molecules are needed for this reaction. Similarly, 6 water molecules are needed for this reaction. So, on the left side of the equation there are a total of 6 carbon atoms, 12 hydrogen atoms, and 18 (12 + 6) oxygen atoms. The carbon dioxide and water molecules are broken apart and the atoms combine to form one sugar molecule and 6 O_2 molecules. On the right side of the equation, there are 6 carbon atoms, 12 hydrogen atoms, and a total of 18 oxygen atoms, just like there were to begin with. The first law of thermodynamics says that matter cannot be created or destroyed; it can only change form. And chemical equations help us to see that even though the product does not look at all like what you started with, the atoms (or amount of matter) were not lost, their form was just changed.

Complete the "Reactants and Products" worksheet to get practice working with different kinds of equations.

Chemical Reactions

Catalysts

Speeding things up

How can we speed up a reaction?

Words to know:

activation energy

enzyme

catalyst

inhibitor

Challenge words:

homogeneous catalyst

heterogeneous catalyst

As we have discussed in previous lessons, some chemical reactions are very quick and others are very slow. The rate at which a chemical reaction takes place depends on several things. What things have you already learned about that affected reaction rate? The temperature of the reactants, the concentration of reactants, and the surface area of the reactants all affect how quickly a reaction will occur. However, there are other factors that affect reaction rate as well. The reactivity of the substances affects how fast the reaction occurs. Reactions involving hydrogen are likely to go more quickly than reactions involving metals because hydrogen is very reactive.

Another factor affecting reaction rates is available energy. In order for many chemical reactions to take place, there must be a certain amount of energy available. Breaking atomic bonds requires energy and creating atomic bonds releases energy. Before a reaction can even begin there has to be enough energy available to break the necessary bonds. This energy is called the **activation energy**. When the activation energy of a reaction is low, the reaction occurs very quickly. When the activation energy is high, it occurs slowly.

The reactants have to reach a certain level of energy, or "height," before they can react with one another. Adding another substance to the mix can sometimes speed up this process. This type of substance is called a **catalyst**. Adding a catalyst is like finding a pass or shortcut over the mountain. It reduces the amount of energy necessary for the reaction to take place.

We already discussed one very important catalyst—chlorophyll. Chlorophyll is a necessary ingredient in plant cells that helps speed up the reaction rate between carbon dioxide and water in the photosynthesis reaction. However, as we learned in the fun fact in the previous lesson, chlorophyll does not show up in the chemical equation because it is not used up in the reaction. A catalyst is something that alters the rate of the reaction without being consumed in the reaction. It is important to remember that a catalyst does not make an impossible reaction possible, it just makes the reaction easier. It can do this in a number of ways.

Some very important catalysts are called enzymes. **Enzymes** are found in living cells and are used in reactions involved in digestion, muscle contraction, cell construction, and reproduction. Without the many enzymes in our bodies, the chemical reactions necessary for life would occur so slowly that we would not be able to live. For example, in digestion starch is broken down into glucose. At normal body temperature, this reaction would take weeks to be completed. However, we cannot wait for weeks for our food to be digested. So God created the α-amylase (alpha amylase) enzyme to be part of our digestive systems. This enzyme makes it so the starch to glucose reaction takes only a few seconds.

Another common enzyme found in many living cells is catalase. Catalase allows the decomposition of hydrogen peroxide into water and oxygen ($2 H_2O_2 \longrightarrow 2H_2O + O_2$) to occur nearly ten billion times faster than it normally would without it. This is very important because hydrogen peroxide, H_2O_2, is a by-product of many cellular metabolic processes. This means that it is produced when your cells produce other needed chemicals. However, hydrogen peroxide is not a useful chemical in your body. So there needs to be a way to break it down into water and oxygen, two compounds that your body needs. Without catalase in your cells to break it down quickly, the levels of hydrogen peroxide would build up and poison your body. But God designed a way for the hydrogen peroxide to be quickly changed to useful compounds.

A catalyst can be very helpful if you wish to increase the rate of a reaction. But what if you want to slow down a reaction that is happening faster than you want it to? Food spoiling is a chemical reaction that we all want to slow down as much

Fun Fact

The metal nickel is a catalyst used in the making of margarine. It is needed in the hydrogenation process that turns liquid vegetable oil into solid margarine.

🧪 Catalysts & inhibitors

Activity 1

Purpose: To observe the catalytic effect of catalase, an enzyme that is present in many living cells

Materials: hydrogen peroxide, potato, drinking glass

Procedure:

1. Pour some hydrogen peroxide into a glass. Observe it for a few minutes. What do you observe happening? (Probably not much)

2. Make a hypothesis about what will happen if you place a slice of potato in the hydrogen peroxide.

3. Place a slice of potato in the peroxide and observe for a few minutes. What do you observe happening? (You should see little bubbles coming up off the potato.)

Conclusion: The potato contains catalase. The catalase is working as a catalyst to break the hydrogen peroxide into water and oxygen. The bubbles you see are the oxygen gas that is being produced. Is this what you predicted would happen?

Activity 2

Purpose: To observe the effects of inhibitors

Materials: apple, lemon juice, knife, brush

Procedure:

1. Slice an apple into quarters.

2. Brush two slices of apple with lemon juice.

3. What do you think will happen to the slices with the lemon juice? What do you think will happen to the slices without the lemon juice?

4. Wait 15 minutes. What differences do you see between the slices with the lemon juice and those without?

Conclusion: You should observe that the uncoated slices are turning brown and the coated slices are not. The acid in lemon juice acts as an inhibitor. It prevents the oxygen molecules from reacting with the apple molecules to produce the brown colored chemical. Other inhibitors are used in foods to prevent them from spoiling. They are often called preservatives on food labels.

as possible. In this case you need a "negative cat-alyst." A "negative catalyst" is called an **inhibitor**. An inhibitor prevents a reaction from occurring by either keeping the reactants apart, or by bonding with one of the reactants so that the chemical reaction cannot take place. ✳

 # What did we learn?

- What is a catalyst?

- How does a catalyst work?

- What is an inhibitor?

- What is an enzyme?

 # Taking it further

- Why is it important that living cells have enzymes?

- Are catalysts always good?

 # Types of catalysts

There are two different kinds of catalysts and they work very differently. First, if the catalyst and the reactants are in the same phase, for example they are both gases or both liquids, then the catalyst is called a **homogeneous catalyst**. Homogeneous catalysts generally work by chemically combining with one of the reactants to form a new substance, which then quickly combines with the other reactant to form the product. An example will make this more clear.

The oxidation of sulfur dioxide is a very slow reaction. It is represented by the chemical equation:

$$2SO_2 + O_2 \rightarrow 2SO_3$$

All of these molecules are gases. To speed up this reaction we can add some nitrogen monoxide gas, NO, in with the reactants. Although the sulfur dioxide will react with the oxygen gas, the nitrogen monoxide reacts with the oxygen much more quickly to form nitrogen dioxide. Below is the chemical equation showing this reaction.

$$2NO + O_2 \rightarrow 2NO_2$$

Now the sulfur dioxide and nitrogen dioxide react very quickly to form the sulfur trioxide gas from the original equation. This reaction looks like this:

$$2NO_2 + 2SO_2 \rightarrow 2SO_3 + 2NO$$

Without the catalyst, you start with sulfur dioxide and oxygen and end up with sulfur trioxide, but it takes a long time for the reaction to occur. With the catalyst, you start with sulfur dioxide, oxygen, and nitrogen monoxide and end up with sulfur trioxide and nitrogen monoxide. The catalyst was used for an intermediate reaction, but was not part of the final product, and you got to the final product much more quickly.

A second kind of catalyst is a **heterogeneous catalyst**. This type of catalyst is one that is in a different phase from the reactants. Commonly the catalyst is a solid and the reactants are gases or liquids. This type of catalyst works in a very different way from the homogeneous catalyst. A heterogeneous catalyst attracts the reactants to itself, forcing them to come closer together. This encourages the reaction to occur more quickly because it increases the probability of the reactants interacting.

One very important use of heterogeneous catalysts is in the design of a catalytic converter. A catalytic converter reduces toxic emissions from your car.

The main reaction taking place inside your car's engine is a combustion reaction. Ideally, the gasoline mixes with the oxygen in the air to produce energy and carbon dioxide. However, the reaction takes place so quickly that there is not always enough oxygen to fully react with the carbon that is released in the combustion, so often carbon monoxide is produced instead of carbon dioxide. Carbon dioxide is harmless for people to breathe, but carbon monoxide is poisonous to breathe.

The catalytic converter is a device on a car through which the car exhaust must flow. The inside of the device is coated with platinum or rhodium. These solid metals attract carbon monoxide molecules and oxygen molecules in the exhaust. Since these molecules are attracted to the metal, they move to the metal surface. This causes them to come closer together than they were in the air. As they get close together the carbon monoxide combines with the oxygen to form carbon dioxide. The metal has reduced the energy required for the reaction by pulling the reactants together and increasing their concentration.

Both homogeneous and heterogeneous catalysts are important in many areas of our lives.

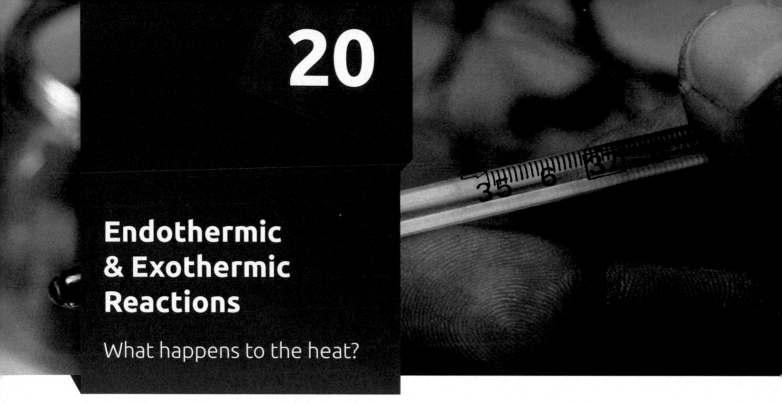

Endothermic & Exothermic Reactions

What happens to the heat?

What kinds of reactions create heat?

Words to know:

endothermic reaction   exothermic reaction

Challenge words:

enthalpy

Energy plays a very important role in chemical reactions. Without the energy from sunlight, photosynthesis cannot occur. The solar energy is stored in the sugar molecules and later released when an animal eats the plant. This storing and releasing of energy is a very important part of God's provision for life on earth.

A chemical reaction that stores energy is called an **endothermic reaction**. Another way to think of an endothermic reaction is to think of it as absorbing energy. The energy goes in; "in" sounds like "en," so endothermic has the energy going into the reaction. In photosynthesis, the energy that is absorbed is in the form of light. However, most endothermic reactions absorb energy in the form of heat. This energy must be added to the reactants in order for the reaction to occur.

One common endothermic reaction occurs when you are baking. Baking soda decomposes with the heat of the oven, releasing carbon dioxide gas. Similarly, yeast reacts much more quickly when heat is added. These are both endothermic reactions. One endothermic reaction you may not associate with heat is a chemical "ice pack." When an athlete is hurt, the doctor or trainer may use a special pack that contains two chemicals that are separated inside the pack. When these chemicals are combined, they absorb heat so the pack feels cool and helps reduce swelling around the injured area.

Not all chemical reactions absorb energy. Many chemical reactions release energy. These reactions are called **exothermic reactions**. You can remember this by thinking that "exo" sounds like "exit." The exit is how you leave a building, and energy is leaving an exothermic reaction. Energy can be released in the form of light or heat.

One of the most common examples of an exothermic reaction is combustion or burning. In one form of combustion, methane gas combines with oxygen to produce carbon dioxide, water, light, and heat. The chemical equation for this reaction is:

$$CH_4 + 2O_2 \longrightarrow CO_2 + 2H_2O$$

This is a similar reaction to the one between gasoline and oxygen in your car's engine.

Endothermic & exothermic reactions

Endothermic reaction

Purpose: To observe the effect of heat on an egg cooking

Materials: five pieces of paper, water, five uncooked eggs, small sauce pan, stove, timer or clock .

Procedure:

1. Label five pieces of paper with the numbers 1–5.

2. Place five uncooked eggs in a small pan.

3. Cover them with water and bring to a boil over medium heat. Begin timing as soon as the water begins to boil.

4. After one minute remove one egg and place it on the paper marked with a 1.

5. One minute later, after a total two minutes of boiling, remove a second egg and place it on the number 2.

6. Continue removing an egg after each minute has passed, placing the egg on the paper showing its total cooking time.

7. After removing all of the eggs, remove the pan from the stove.

8. Break open each egg and you will be able to observe how the molecules in the egg have reacted as the heat was added to them.

Exothermic reaction

One reaction that produces or releases heat is the formation of rust, called oxidation. This occurs in small amounts and is not usually noticeable. However, you can measure the heat released in a sealed container.

Purpose: To measure heat released by oxidation

Materials: steel wool, jar with lid, thermometer, vinegar

Procedure:

1. Place a piece of steel wool, the kind without soap in it, in a jar.

2. Place a thermometer in the jar so that you can read the temperature in the jar.

3. Seal the jar and wait 5 minutes. Read the temperature inside the jar.

4. Next, open the jar and pour ¼ cup of room temperature vinegar over the steel. The acid in the vinegar and the oxygen in the air will react with the steel to form rust.

5. Reseal the jar and measure the temperature inside the jar every five minutes for twenty minutes. What did you observe? You should see the temperature in the jar rise as the chemical reaction releases heat.

The heat produced by combustion can be helpful if you are trying to heat your house, such as when you burn natural gas in your furnace. But in a car engine, too much heat can be harmful to the engine. Therefore, the engine must be cooled. This is most often done by running water from the radiator around the engine to absorb the heat.

Another very important exothermic reaction is the reaction that occurs as your food is digested. The energy released as food molecules are broken down is necessary for you to be able to function. The heat released helps your body regulate its temperature. Warm-blooded animals generally have to eat more food than cold-blooded animals in order to regulate their body temperatures. ✳

What did we learn?

- What is an exothermic reaction?
- What is an endothermic reaction?

Taking it further

- If a chemical reaction produces a spark, is it likely to be an endothermic or exothermic reaction?

- How do photosynthesis and digestion reveal God's plan for life?

- If the temperature of the product is lower than the temperature of the reactants, was the reaction endothermic or exothermic?

Energy in a reaction

Endothermic and exothermic reactions are all about energy: energy entering the substance that is formed or energy exiting the substance that is formed. But where does this energy come from? With an endothermic reaction it may be somewhat obvious where the energy is coming from. If the air around the reaction becomes colder during the reaction, it is obvious that heat is being removed from the air. However, other reactions are not so obvious. Photosynthesis is an endothermic reaction, but the temperature around a leaf does not go down as it performs photosynthesis. Instead its energy comes from the light of the sun.

As an endothermic reaction takes place, where does the energy go? We know that according to the first law of thermodynamics energy cannot be created or destroyed; so we know the energy is not lost, it has just changed form. What form is the energy in now? The energy is stored in the bonds of the products.

All chemical bonds between atoms contain energy. Some bonds are strong and store a greater amount of energy than weaker bonds. Recall that it takes energy to break bonds. It takes more energy to break strong bonds than it does to break weak bonds.

Also recall that energy is released when bonds are formed. When weak bonds are formed a small amount of energy is released. When strong bonds are formed more energy is released. This energy is usually released as either heat or light.

So, when a chemical reaction takes place some energy is required to break the bonds of the reactants. The amount of energy required depends on how many bonds must be broken and how strong those bonds are. Then as the products are formed the new bonds release energy. Again the amount of energy released depends on how many bonds are formed and how strong those bonds are. If the amount of energy required to break the bonds in the reactants is greater than the amount of energy released by the bonds formed in the products, then the reaction is endothermic. If the amount of energy released is

Fireworks are the result of an exothermic reaction that produces light, heat, and sound.

greater than the amount required to break the bonds then the reaction is exothermic.

The amount of energy stored in a substance's bonds is called its **enthalpy** (EN-thal-pee). Many scientific experiments have been conducted to determine the enthalpy contained in various compounds. These values can be found in chemistry charts. To determine if a chemical reaction is endothermic or exothermic, scientists do not have to test the temperature of the surroundings. Instead, they can calculate the enthalpy of all of the reactants and the enthalpy of all of the products and decide if the enthalpy is higher before or after the reaction. If the enthalpy of the reactants is higher than the enthalpy of the products, then energy was released and the reaction was exothermic. If the enthalpy of the reactants is less than the enthalpy of the products, then energy was absorbed during the reaction and it was endothermic.

Now you get to do an experiment to determine if a reaction is endothermic or exothermic. Perform the experiment described on the "Endothermic or Exothermic?" worksheet.

UNIT 5

Acids & Bases

◊ **Distinguish** between the properties of acids and bases.

◊ **Describe** the result of mixing acids and bases.

◊ **Demonstrate** how to test for acids and bases.

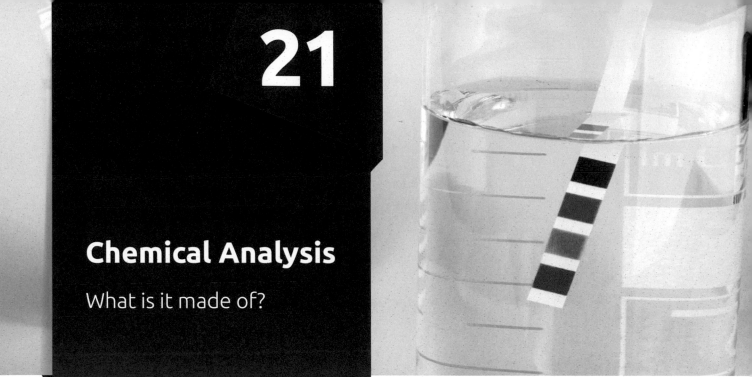

21

Chemical Analysis

What is it made of?

What kinds of chemical tests are there?

Words to know:

chemical analysis   pH scale

indicator

How can you know what chemicals a sub-stance contains? A good scientist always starts with observation. You can tell many things about a sample by observing its color, texture, state, mass, boiling and freezing points, and other physical characteristics. However, tasting and smelling chemicals can be very dangerous. Touching can also be dangerous as some chemicals are corrosive and can burn your skin. So direct observation of physical characteristics is limited. Therefore, often the most useful way to determine what kind of matter a sample is made of is to test it with chemical reactions. This type of testing is called **chemical analysis.**

Some chemical analysis techniques can be very involved and require a greater understanding of chemistry than we will cover in this book. Others are dangerous and should only be done in a laboratory. For example, one type of chemical analysis is called a flame test. A small sample of the substance is heated until it burns. The color of the flame can indicate what elements were in the sample. Other tests require expensive equipment. A spectroscope is a piece of equipment that passes a spectrum of light through a sample. The color of light that passes through indicates what the sample is made of. Although these tests are interesting, they are not easy to do at home. Fortunately, there are some chemical analysis tests that are fun and easy to do at home.

One common type of chemical test that is easy to do is to use indicators. An indicator is a chemical compound that changes color when it reacts with

A flame test

certain other chemicals. Iodine is a liquid that is normally red or orange-brown. But in the presence of starch, iodine reacts to form a liquid that is blue or green. This is a simple way to test if your sample contains starch. Other chemicals change color when they are in the presence of protein or sugar. Indicators are an important part of chemical analysis.

One of the most common uses of indicators is to test for acids and bases. There are several chemicals that change color in the presence of an acid or a base. One of the most famous is litmus. Litmus is a chemical produced from certain lichens that are native to California. Litmus is naturally blue but it turns red in the presence of an acid. Blue litmus paper is thus used to test for acids in liquids. Once the paper turns red it stays red until it reacts with a base. Then it becomes blue again. So red litmus paper can be used to test for a base.

Other chemicals turn different colors depending on the strength or weakness of the acid or base.

pH indicator paper

These chemicals can be dried together on one sheet of paper to form what is called a universal pH indicator paper, or mixed together to form a universal indicator liquid. The pH scale, which stands for per hydronium, or power of hydrogen, indicates the strength of the acid or base. The pH scale goes from 0 to 14 with 0 being a very strong acid, 7 being neutral (neither acid nor base), and 14 being a very strong base. The universal indicator will change many different colors depending on the strength of the acid or base. One color would indicate a pH of 1, a different color would be a pH of 2, and so on.

If it is not critical to know the strength of an acid or base, other chemicals can be used just to indicate the presence of acids and bases. Bromothymol blue is a substance that is blue in basic solutions, green

Fun Fact

Stomach acid is hydrochloric acid (HCl) and can be a 1 on the pH scale—a very strong acid. Lye, which is used in some cleaners and is sometimes used in soap, is a strong base and can be a 14 on the pH scale. Pure water, blood, and eggs are a 7 on the pH scale; they are neutral.

🧪 Making an acid/base indicator

Purpose: To make your own acid/base indicator solution

Materials: purple cabbage, water, microwave oven or sauce pan and stove

Procedure:

1. Combine 1 cup of chopped purple cabbage with 1 cup of water.

2. Heat in the microwave for 2–3 minutes or bring water to a boil and boil for 5 minutes on the stove.

3. Drain and save the water. The water should have a definite purple color. If the water is very light, add it back in with the cabbage and boil for a few more minutes.

4. Store your indicator in a sealed container and keep it in the refrigerator for future use.

Conclusion: The purple pigment from the cabbage chemically reacts with acids to form a pink liquid, and it chemically reacts with bases to form a blue or blue/green liquid. If the substance is neutral, the indicator will remain purple. Use your new indicator to test several substances around the house to see if they are acids, bases, or neutral by combining a few drops of indicator with the substance to be tested. The substance to be tested must be a liquid or a solid that is dissolved in water.

Fun Fact

Hydrangeas are flowering plants. If the soil that the plant is growing in is acidic, the flowers will be blue. If the soil is basic, the flowers will be pink. Soil formed from chalk or limestone tends to be basic and soil formed from sandstone tends to be acidic.

in neutral solutions, and yellow in acidic solutions. Several plants can also be used to make acid/base indicators. One of the easiest to use is red cabbage. The liquid that is drained after boiling red or purple cabbage is purple. In the presence of an acid, it will turn pink and in the presence of a base it will turn blue or green.

Chemical analysis is very useful and can be fun. In the next few lessons, we will use an acid/base indicator to learn more about the chemicals around us. ✳

 # What did we learn?

- What is chemical analysis?
- List three different types of chemical analysis.
- What is a chemical indicator?
- What is the pH scale?
- What does a pH of 7 tell you about a substance?

 # Taking it further

- Why is it important to periodically test the pH of swimming pool water?
- Name at least one other use for testing pH of a liquid.

 # Chemical analysis methods

There are a variety of chemical analysis methods that are used today. Choose one of the methods listed here. Do some research and see what you can find out about that analysis method. How does it work? What does it tell you? What equipment do you need to do it? Make a presentation of what you have learned.

- Spectroscopy
- Mass Spectrometry
- Colorimetry
- Chromatography
- Electrophoresis
- Crystallography
- Microscopy
- Electrochemistry
- Gravimetry

22

Acids

Does it burn?

What makes a substance an acid?

Words to know:

acid

neutralize

hydronium ion

Challenge words:

electroplating

What do you think of when you hear the word acid? Do you picture a liquid eating through metal and destroying everything in its path? Some acids are very caustic and can eat through metals; however, many acids are weak and are used every day. Let's take a look at what an acid actually is.

Acids and bases are substances that form ions when dissolved in water. Recall that ions are molecules or atoms that have either a positive or negative charge. When an **acid** is dissolved in water, one or more hydrogen atoms break off of the molecule. The original molecule holds tightly to the electrons so the hydrogen atom leaves behind its electron, causing the hydrogen to have a positive charge and the remaining molecule to have a negative charge.

The symbol for a positive hydrogen atom is H^+. The H^+ ion is really just a proton. It is very reactive and won't stay alone for very long. It quickly combines with a water molecule to form H_3O^+, which is called a **hydronium ion**. The formation of hydronium ions in water is what classifies a substance as an acid. Some acids are stronger than others. A strong acid easily gives up its hydrogen atoms to form hydronium ions and a weak acid holds onto most of its hydrogen atoms so it forms fewer hydronium ions.

Acids have specific characteristics. The word *acid* comes from the Latin word *acer* meaning sour, and foods that contain acids have a distinct sour taste. Citrus fruits have citric acid in them, which is why lemons and limes have such a sour flavor. Soft

Fun Fact

A bee sting contains formic acid. When the acid combines with the water in your skin cells it forms hydronium ions, which irritate or hurt your cells. You can help neutralize the acid from the bee sting by covering the area with a paste made from baking soda and water or with toothpaste, both of which are bases.

Lemons taste sour because of the citric acid in them.

drinks containing carbon dioxide form carbonic acid, which gives the soda a sour/tangy flavor. Foods that contain vinegar, such as pickles, are sour because of the acetic acid from the vinegar. And rhubarb contains oxalic acid, giving it a sour taste as well.

Acids also have other distinctive characteristics. Because acids easily form ions, they are good conductors of electricity. Most acids will react with

Fun Fact

Sulfuric acid is the most produced chemical in the United States. The biggest use of sulfuric acid is in the making of fertilizers. It is also used to make car batteries, paints, plastics, and many other manufactured items. In fact, sulfuric acid is so important to manufacturing that some economists use a country's use of sulfuric acid as an indicator of how well that country's economy is doing.

metals and many are corrosive and can burn your skin. Acids **neutralize** bases, meaning they react with them to form substances that are neither acid nor base. And finally, acids react with indicators. As discussed in the previous lesson, acids change the color of many different compounds when they are chemically combined.

Acids are found in many places other than food. Hydrochloric acid is found in your stomach and helps to digest your food. Sulfuric acid is used in car batteries. And decaying plants produce humic acid. So, the next time you hear the word *acid*, you don't have to fear a liquid that melts through everything it touches. Just think about your favorite soft drink. ✳

What did we learn?

- What defines a substance as an acid?
- What is a hydronium ion?
- How is a weak acid different from a strong acid?
- What are some common characteristics of an acid?
- How can you tell if a substance is an acid?

Taking it further

- Why is saliva slightly acidic?
- Would you expect water taken from a puddle on the forest floor to be acidic, neutral, or basic? Why?
- What would you expect to be a key ingredient in sour candy?

🧪 Testing for acids

Purpose: To test for acids

Materials: lemon juice, vinegar, clear soda, milk, saliva, cabbage indicator solution from lesson 21

Procedure:

1. Add a few drops of the indicator you made in the previous lesson to a sample of each of the following items to determine if they are acids.

- Lemon juice
- Vinegar
- Clear soda pop—lemon lime soda works well
- Milk
- Saliva

Questions:

- What color did the indicator become when mixed with each of these items?
- Which items are acidic?

🏅 Displacement reaction

Acids and bases have many uses in industry. They can be used for many chemical reactions. Today you will use an acid to move copper atoms from a penny to a steel paperclip. The acid reacts with the copper in the penny and with the iron in the paperclip. This is a displacement reaction so the iron is displaced by the copper.

Purpose: To create a copper-coated paperclip

Materials: 15 pennies, jar with lid, salt, vinegar, steel paperclip

Procedure:

1. Put 15 pennies into a jar.

2. Sprinkle 2 tablespoons of salt over the pennies.

3. Add enough vinegar to cover the pennies.

4. Put a lid on the jar and swirl the solution for 15 seconds. Try to have the pennies end up on top of the salt.

5. Open the jar and drop in a steel paper clip. Close the lid.

6. Observe the pennies and the paperclip after 15 minutes. How do they look? What do you observe happening in the jar? Observe them again after 30 minutes and again after 60 minutes.

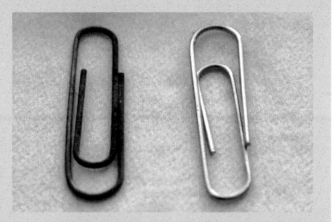

7. Allow the solution to sit undisturbed for several days, then remove the pennies and the paperclip. How do they look compared to when they went into the jar?

Conclusion: This process is similar to the process of electroplating. **Electroplating** is the process of passing electrical current through a metallic salt solution to deposit a thin layer of metal onto a conductive object. This can be done for many reasons. Often electroplating is performed to deposit a layer of metal that will not rust onto a steel object to keep it from rusting. You could speed up this process in your experiment if you connected a penny to one terminal of a battery and the paperclip to the other terminal, while the objects are in the acid solution.

Acids & Bases

23

Bases

The opposite of acids

What makes a substance a base?

Words to know:

base   hydroxide ion

Challenge words:

quantitative   acid/base titration
    measurement

A base is often described as the opposite of an acid, but what does that really mean? Just as an acid produces ions in a water solution, so also a base produces ions in a water solution. But an acid produces positive hydronium ions and a **base** produces negative hydroxide ions. When a substance that is a base is dissolved in water, it releases OH⁻ ions from its molecule, leaving the rest of the original molecule short one electron, so it has a positive charge and consists of one oxygen atom and one hydrogen atom. It pulls an extra electron with it when it leaves the original base molecule. This gives it a negative charge. Therefore, it is called an ion instead of a molecule. The OH⁻ ion is called a **hydroxide ion**. The hydroxide ion is very reactive.

Just as the ability to produce hydronium ions determines the strength of an acid, so also the ability to produce hydroxide ions determines the strength of a base. The more hydroxide ions a base produces in water, the stronger the base. Weak bases hold onto their OH⁻ ions more tightly than strong bases do.

Another name for a base is an alkali. This is because some of the strongest bases are formed from the alkali and alkaline earth metal elements. These are the elements in columns IA and IIA on the periodic table. These elements include sodium, potassium, and calcium.

Because of their common molecular structures, bases have common characteristics. One characteristic of a base is that bases have a bitter taste. Soap is a base and anyone who has ever gotten soap in his mouth can attest to its bitter aftertaste. Bases also have a slippery feeling. And because bases produce ions in water, they are good conductors of electricity. Many bases are also caustic. A strong base can burn your skin as easily as a strong acid can.

Fun Fact

Sodium hydroxide is a base that dissolves wood resin. It is added to wood pulp because it eliminates the resin, leaving the cellulose behind. The cellulose strands are then used to make paper.

🧪 Testing for bases

Purpose: To test for bases

Materials: soap, ammonia, baking soda, anti-acid, toothpaste, cabbage indicator

Procedure:

1. Use the cabbage indicator from the previous lessons to test for bases. Add a few drops of indicator to a sample of each of the following items to determine if they are bases.

- Soap
- Ammonia
- Anti-acid (liquid or tablets that are crushed and dissolved in water)
- Baking Soda
- Toothpaste

Questions:

- What color did the indicator become when mixed with each of these items?
- Which items were bases?

Bases, such as soap, are slippery.

Some common bases you may encounter include ammonium hydroxide, which is found in many household cleaners; sodium hydroxide, which is lye; and magnesium hydroxide, which is found in anti-acid medications. The reason bases are used in anti-acid medications is that an acid and a base will neutralize each other. The H^+ from the acid will quickly combine with the OH^- from the base to form water. Another place you are likely to find a base is in your toothpaste. Your saliva naturally has acids in it that help digest your food, so toothpastes usually have a base in them to help neutralize the acid in your mouth to help prevent tooth decay. ✳

🧠 What did we learn?

- What defines a substance as a base?
- What is a hydroxide ion?
- How is a weak base different from a strong base?
- What are some common characteristics of a base?
- How can you tell if a substance is a base?

🚀 Taking it further

- If you spill a base, what should you do before trying to clean it up?
- Do you think that strontium (Sr) is likely to form a strong base? Why or why not?

Fun Fact

A wasp sting contains a base. When the hydroxide ions in the base irritate or hurt your cells, you can help neutralize the alkali from the wasp sting by covering the area with vinegar. But be sure that it is a wasp that has stung you and not a bee. Bee stings contain an acid and vinegar will only increase the problem, not neutralize it.

Acids & Bases

Acid/base titration

Although you have tested for the presence of acids and bases using your indicator, you have not done any **quantitative measurements**, tests that use actual numbers to measure how much of something there is. **Acid/base titration** is a method for determining the unknown quantity of a base (or acid) by carefully measuring the exact amount of acid (or base) needed to completely neutralize it. This may sound complicated, but an example may help show how easy this is.

If you know how many molecules of acid are in a drop of acid, and you know how many drops of acid it takes to neutralize a base solution, then you know how many molecules of base were in the solution. Learning how to calculate the number of molecules in a sample is beyond the scope of this book; you will learn how to do this in a high school chemistry course. For now, just think of titration as a way to figure out how many drops of base are in a solution by counting how many drops of acid are needed to neutralize it.

Purpose: To better understand how acid/base titration works

Materials: distilled water, clear glass, ammonia, acid/base indicator, vinegar, eyedropper

Procedure:

1. Pour ½ cup of distilled water into a clear glass.

2. Add 2 teaspoons of clear ammonia.

3. Next add one tablespoon of the acid/base indicator. This should result in a blue/green solution.

4. Now use an eyedropper to add vinegar to this solution one drop at a time until you see the solution just start to turn a pale pink. Count the drops as you add them to the solution. This will take a while so don't get impatient.

Conclusion: When the solution turns pink, it indicates that there are no more base molecules for the acid to react with so it is now reacting with the indicator. The number of drops of vinegar gives you an indication of the number of drops of ammonia in the solution. Actual titration involves chemical formulas and calculation of the number of molecules, but you get the basic idea of titration here.

Acids & Bases

24

Salts

Pass the salt, please.

What are salts, and how are they formed?

Words to know:

salt

normal salt

acid salt

basic salt

Challenge words:

proton donor

proton acceptor

What do you think of when someone says, "Pass the salt, please"? You would probably think of table salt. But sodium chloride, table salt, is not the only salt around. There are many other common salts. A few of these salts are used in cooking. For

example MSG, monosodium glutamate, is a salt that is used in many oriental dishes. Other salts are used to make fertilizer, medical supplies, and a number of other chemical products.

A salt is formed when an acid and a base mix. Recall that when an acidic material is dissolved in water the molecule breaks up into a positive hydrogen ion (H^+) and a negative acid ion. Similarly, when a base is dissolved the molecule breaks up into a negative hydroxide (OH^-) ion and a positive base ion. We already discussed how the hydrogen ion and the hydroxide ion combine to form water. But the positive base ion and the negative acid ion also combine to form a salt. For example, table salt is formed when a positive sodium ion, Na^+, combines with a negative chlorine ion, Cl^-, to form $NaCl$. Monosodium glutamate is formed when Na^+ combines with the glutamate ion, $C_5H_8O_4^-$, to form $NaC_5H_8O_4$.

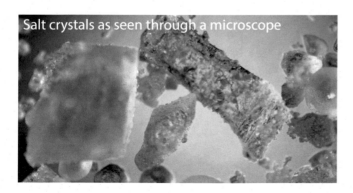

Salt crystals as seen through a microscope

Fun Fact

Many paints receive their color from salts that are added. Vermilion is a salt that is added to make a red paint; cadmium sulfide makes a yellow paint; and malachite is a salt used in some green paints.

When an acid and base completely neutralize each other, the resulting salt is called a **normal salt**. However, not all acids and bases completely neutralize each other. If some of the acid remains after all the base is used up, the result is called an **acid salt**. If all of the acid is used up in the reaction but some of the base remains, the result is called a **basic salt**.

Because of their ionic structures, salts generally form crystals. If you examine table salt, you will see that it forms distinct crystal shapes. This is true of most salts. Another characteristic of most salts is the distinctive salty flavor.

Families of salts are named by the acid from which they originate. Sulfates are salts that are made from sulfuric acid. Chlorides come from hydrochloric acid. Nitrates are formed from nitric acid and carbonates come from carbonic acid. You may have heard of some of these salts and not realized what they were. Many fertilizers contain nitrates, phosphates, and potash, which are all salts.

The next time you salt your corn on the cob, remember that there are many different kinds of salt.

What did we learn?

- How is a salt formed?
- What are two common characteristics of salts?
- How are salt families named?
- Name three salt families.

🚀 Taking it further

- What do you expect to be the results of combining vinegar and lye?
- Why are some salts still acidic or basic?

Fun Fact

Plaster of Paris, that white powder that is used for many art projects, is actually a salt—calcium sulfate.

Acids & Bases

Acid + base = salt + water

When an acid reacts with a base it produces a salt and water. It can also produce other substances such as carbon dioxide. You are going to demonstrate this with an acid/base reaction that you are very familiar with—vinegar and baking soda. Vinegar contains acetic acid which combines with baking soda, which is a base, to produce sodium acetate, which is a salt, as well as water and carbon dioxide. The chemical equation for this reaction is:

$$CH_3COOH + NaHCO_3 \rightarrow CH_3COONa + H_2O + CO_2$$

Acetic acid + baking soda $\rightarrow$ sodium acetate + water + carbon dioxide

Purpose: To demonstrate that an acid and base reaction produces salt and water

Materials: water, measuring cups and spoons, vinegar, baking soda, cup, cotton swabs

Procedure:

1. Place ½ cup of water in a measuring cup. Add 1 teaspoon of baking soda and stir until the solution becomes clear.

2. Pour 1 tablespoon of the solution in a separate cup.

3. Pour 1 tablespoon of vinegar in the measuring cup with the soda water. Stir the solution until the production of bubbles slows down. Stop stirring and wait for the bubbles to stop completely. You now have two solutions. In one cup you have a solution of baking soda and water. This is a basic solution. In the measuring cup you have a solution that was created when the baking soda reacted with the acetic acid in the vinegar. Which solution do you think will have a saltier taste?

4. Use a swab to place a small amount of the soda water solution on your tongue. Think about how salty this solution is. Use a second swab to place a small amount of the vinegar/soda water solution on your tongue. How salty is this solution compared to the first solution?

Conclusion: You should find that the first solution with baking soda and water is slightly salty. However, after adding the vinegar the new solution should taste even saltier since the chemical reaction produced a salt in addition to water and carbon dioxide.

Acid/base reactions

You have learned that an acid is defined by how easily it gives up a hydrogen ion and a base is defined by how easily it gives up a hydronium ion, but there is an alternative way to define acids and bases. Recall that a hydrogen ion (H^+) is really just a proton. So an alternative definition for an acid is a **proton donor** and an alternative definition for a base is a **proton acceptor**. Using this definition, a base does not necessarily have to donate a hydronium ion but has to be able to bond with a hydrogen atom.

Now that you have learned about acid/base reactions and chemical equations it is time for you to put what you have learned to work. Show how well you understand these reactions by completing the "Acid/Base Reactions" worksheet.

Acids & Bases

Batteries

What do an eel, a ray, an African catfish, and the Energizer bunny's battery have in common? They all create electricity by chemical means. It is known that chemicals have been used to generate electricity since Alessandro Volta produced the first modern battery in 1800. Volta discovered that stacks of copper and zinc that were separated by a saltwater solution would create electricity. This early electrochemical cell, or battery, was called a voltaic cell in honor of Volta, and is the basis for all the batteries to follow.

However, it is unclear if Alessandro Volta's batteries were the first batteries ever used in history. In 1938 a German archaeologist, Wilhelm Konig, was working in Khujut Rabu, just outside Baghdad, Iraq. In the artifacts he found a clay jar that measured about five inches (13 cm) long. Inside the jar was a copper cylinder that encased an iron rod. The copper tube and iron rod were held in place with asphalt, but only the iron rod was exposed on the top. It has been shown that if the jar were filled with an electrolyte, like vinegar or wine, a small voltage would be generated between the copper and iron.

This clay jar, and other similar jars, have been dated as early as 200 BC. It is unclear what their purpose might have been. Not all scientists agree that they were used as batteries or to generate electricity. If they were used to generate electricity, they may have been used for medical purposes, or by hooking several of them together they might have generated enough power to electroplate a very thin layer of gold onto silver. So far, the purpose or uses of these *Baghdad batteries*, as they have been called, have not been found in any writings from the past and remain a mystery. So it is commonly accepted that Volta invented the first real battery.

At the heart of every battery is the electrolyte solution. An electrolyte is any solution that conducts electricity. Electricity is conducted by ions or charged particles, so solutions containing acids, bases, or salts make good electrolytes.

In order to conduct electricity, a chemical reaction must take place inside the battery. A simple battery has a center core made out of graphite, which has a positive charge and is attached to the top of the battery. This core is surrounded by an electrolyte paste. The bottom of the battery is attached to a plate of zinc with a negative charge. When the positive and negative terminals are connected, electricity flows from the negative to the positive terminal through the electrolyte paste as a chemical reaction takes place.

Different types of batteries use different metals and different electrolytes, but the idea is the same.

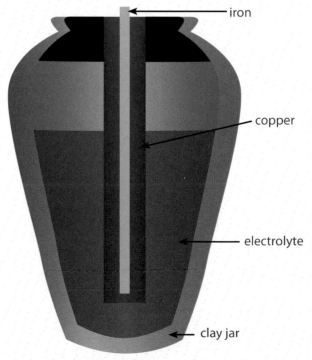

Baghdad battery

A very common example is the car battery, often called a lead-acid battery. In a car battery, negative plates made of lead (Pb) are connected to the anode, or negative terminal, of the battery. The positive plates made of lead dioxide (PbO_2), are connected to the cathode, or positive terminal. These plates are submerged in a sulfuric acid solution (H_2SO_4). When the two terminals are connected, the lead loses two electrons and becomes Pb^{2+}. This atom combines with an SO_4^{2-} ion in the solution to produce $PbSO_4$ (lead sulfate). At the cathode, PbO_2 atoms combine with the H_2 atoms in the electrolyte solution to form Pb (lead) and H_2O (water). This chemical reaction aids in the flow of electrons through the electrolyte solution, which produces electricity that helps start your car.

In recent years, many new designs of rechargeable batteries have been developed. The batteries are recharged by applying a higher voltage in the opposite direction. This causes the chemical reaction to reverse and the battery can again produce electricity.

The next time you replace the batteries in your flashlight, remember that you are holding a chemical reaction in your hand.

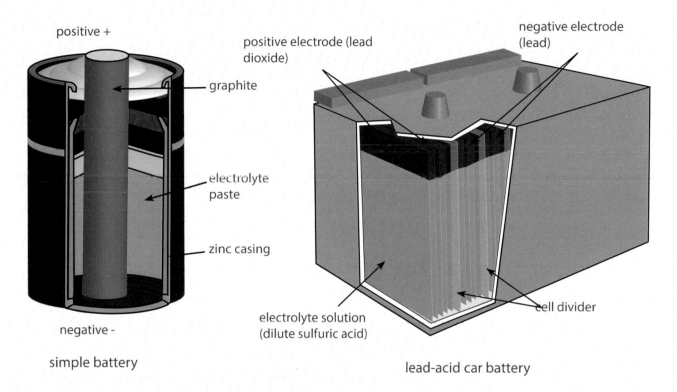

positive +

positive electrode (lead dioxide)

negative electrode (lead)

graphite

electrolyte paste

zinc casing

negative -

simple battery

electrolyte solution (dilute sulfuric acid)

cell divider

lead-acid car battery

UNIT 6

Biochemistry

◊ **Describe** the importance of water, proteins, fats, and carbohydrates to living things.

◊ **Explain** the connection between natural decomposers and fertilizers.

◊ **Describe** how medicines have impacted mankind.

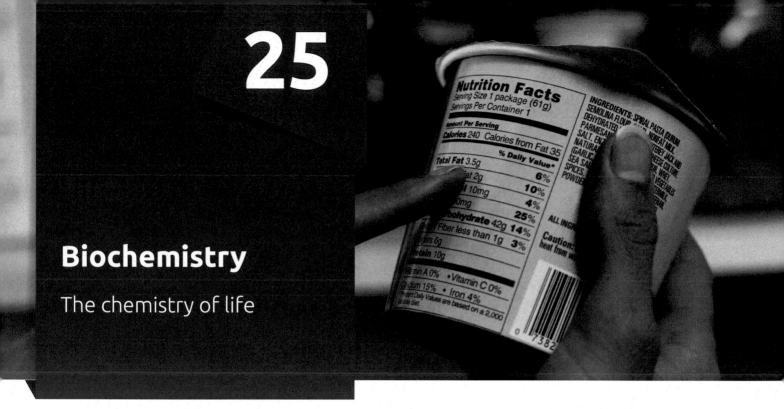

25

Biochemistry

The chemistry of life

How do our bodies use chemistry?

Words to know:

solvent

protein

fat

carbohydrate

Challenge words:

protease

Plants and animals depend on chemical reactions for nearly every function of life. As you have already learned, plants carry on the chemical reaction of photosynthesis, converting water and carbon dioxide into sugar and oxygen, thus providing food for nearly every food chain. Cellular respiration is the chemical reaction that breaks down the sugar into carbon dioxide, water, and energy for the body. Another important chemical reaction that takes place in nearly every animal occurs during breathing. The hemoglobin in the red blood cells reacts with the oxygen in the lungs. This new compound is carried by the blood stream to all parts of the body where it reacts with the muscles to release the oxygen and make it available for other uses, such as cellular respiration.

Chemical reactions are taking place in your body all the time. Most of these chemical reactions require water as a **solvent**. God designed the plasma in your blood to be mostly water, which is used to dissolve the many chemical compounds that your body needs so they can be easily transported throughout your body. About two-thirds of

Our bodies need about ½ gallon of water each day to function properly.

A balanced diet

Because your body needs particular chemicals to function, it is necessary that you eat a well-balanced diet. You need to be sure to include carbohydrates, proteins, and fats each day. To help you in deciding what to eat, food manufacturers include information on food labels that tell you how much of each of these chemicals you will get in a serving. The labels also tell how many calories are in a serving so you know how much energy the food contains. And because some people must watch their sodium intake, most food labels include the amount of sodium as well. Examine the label shown here to see what information is included.

According to the USDA (United States Department of Agriculture), each day everyone should eat foods from each of the following food groups: grains, fruits, vegetables, dairy, and meat. This is because the various food groups are composed of the different chemicals your body needs. Grains, fruits, and vegetables have the different carbohydrates your body needs. Dairy products and meats primarily have proteins and fats.

Americans often eat foods high in fat and don't eat enough fruits and vegetables. Note that many pre-packaged foods contain a large amount of fat and salt—often more than your body needs. Fresh foods that you prepare yourself are generally healthier for you. Design a well-balanced meal that includes all the necessary chemicals to help your body stay healthy.

Nutrition Facts

Serving Size 1 Package (42.5g)

Amount Per Serving

Calories 220 Calories from Fat 110

	% Daily Value*
Total Fat 12g	18%
Saturated Fat 11g	55%
Trans Fat 0g	
Cholesterol 0mg	0%
Sodium 50mg	2%
Total Carbohydrate 29g	10%
Dietary Fiber less than 1g	4%
Sugars 24g	
Protein 1g	

Vitamin A 0%	•	Vitamin C 0%
Calcium 0%	•	Iron 2%

* Percent Daily Values are based on a 2,000 calorie diet. Your daily values may be higher or lower depending on your calorie needs:

	Calories	2,000	2,500
Total Fat	Less than	65g	80g
Sat. Fat	Less than	20g	25g
Cholesterol	Less than	300mg	300mg
Sodium	Less than	2,400mg	2,400mg
Total Carbohydrate		300g	375g
Dietary Fiber		25g	30g

your body weight is water. This is about 70 pints (33 l) of fluid in an average person.

Because water is so vital to most chemical functions in your body, it is necessary to make sure you drink enough water to replace the water used each day. Most people need about 4.4 pints (2 l) of water each day. On average, 1.2 pints (0.6 l) of water come from the food you eat, 2.6 pints (1.2 l) come from the liquids you drink, and the chemical processes that take place in your body produce about 0.5 pints (0.2 l) of water. This should equal the amount of water you lose each day through urine, feces, sweat, and breathing.

The major chemicals that are used by your body are **proteins, fats,** and **carbohydrates**. (These are discussed in depth in the book, *Properties of Matter*.) In order to be able to use these chemicals, your body produces over 50 different chemicals that are used in digestion. Most of these chemicals are enzymes, which are catalysts that are used to speed up the digestion process. Most of these chemicals are supplied by the gall bladder, liver, and pancreas. The chemical processes of digestion start in the mouth where the enzyme salivary amylase reacts with starch to break the starch molecules into sugar molecules. Once the food reaches the stomach, chemicals are added that break down proteins and fats into smaller molecules. In the small intestine, more chemicals are added to break the smaller protein molecules down into amino acids, and also break complex sugars into simple sugars. These simple sugars are then transported to all the cells in your body where cellular respiration occurs, breaking the sugars apart to release the stored energy and produce CO_2 and water.

Biochemistry

There are many other chemical reactions taking place in your body besides the ones required for breathing and digestion. Your body releases chemicals called hormones which tell your body how to grow and how to change as you grow up. Your body also releases chemicals that make you sleepy at bedtime and chemicals that help you feel awake in the morning. Your body is an amazing chemical factory. ✳

 # What did we learn?

- List at least two chemical functions performed inside living creatures.
- What is the chemical reaction that takes place during photosynthesis?
- What is the main chemical reaction that takes place during digestion?
- What substance is necessary for nearly every chemical reaction in living things?
- Name the three major chemicals your body needs that are found in the foods we eat.

 # Taking it further

- Why did God design your body to have enzymes?
- With what you know about chemical processes, why do you think it is important to brush your teeth after you eat?
- Can you think of other chemical processes in your body besides the ones mentioned in this lesson?

Fun Fact

Each day your body produces about 12 pints (5.6 l) of digestion fluids. This includes 2.6 pints (1.2 l) of saliva, 1.7 pints (0.8 l) of bile, 2.6 pints (1.2 l) of pancreatic juice, and 5.1 pints (2.4 l) of intestinal juices. Most of the fluid in these liquids is recycled throughout your body.

 # Enzymes

Enzymes are critical to the chemical functions that are happening in living organisms so it is important that they be able to do their jobs. Several factors affect the rate at which enzymes work. What factors have you learned about that affect reaction rates of chemical reactions in general? You have learned that temperature, density, and surface area of the reactants, and the presence of catalysts and inhibitors can all affect the rate of a chemical reaction. There are similar things that affect how effective enzymes are at speeding up a chemical reaction. Two of these factors are temperature and pH (how acidic or basic the surrounding tissues are).

Many of the enzymes that are in your body can be found in plants as well. One enzyme that works to break down protein is called **protease**. This enzyme is found in several fruits including pineapple, kiwi, and papaya. Today you are going to do an experiment using fresh pineapple juice to demonstrate the effects of temperature and pH on protease.

Gelatin is mostly made of protein. This is what causes the gelatin to set or become thick. If you add protease to gelatin it will break down the protein and the gelatin will not set. If protease becomes too hot or is in a very acidic environment it will be destroyed. The following experiment will show how temperature and acid affect protease.

Purpose: To demonstrate the effects of temperature and pH on protease

Materials: box of gelatin mix, fresh pineapple (do not use canned or frozen), vinegar, four cups, measuring spoon, stove, sauce pan, refrigerator, "Enzyme Reaction" worksheet

Procedure:

1. Peel and cut up a fresh pineapple. Place some of the fruit in a blender and blend until you have a pulpy liquid.

2. Label four cups with the numbers 1–4.

3. Place 1 tablespoon of pineapple juice/pulp in cup number 1.

4. Place 1 tablespoon of pineapple juice/pulp and 1 tablespoon of vinegar in cup 2. Stir to mix the two liquids.

5. Using a clean spoon, place the rest of the pineapple juice in a sauce pan. Heat on medium heat on the stove until the liquid has boiled for 5 minutes. Using a clean measuring spoon, place 1 tablespoon of the heated juice/pulp in cup 3. It is very important that none of the raw pineapple juice or vinegar are mixed in with this heated juice.

6. In a bowl, prepare the gelatin according to the package directions. Pour ½ cup of the gelatin into each of the four cups. Place all four cups in the refrigerator.

7. Complete the hypothesis section of the "Enzyme Reaction" worksheet.

8. Observe each cup of gelatin after 30 minutes. Write your observations of how the gelatin looks on the worksheet.

9. Repeat your observations after 60 minutes, 90 minutes, 2 hours, and 3 hours.

10. At the end of 3 hours answer the questions on the worksheet.

Pineapples contain the enzyme protease.

Conclusion: You should have found that the liquid in cup 1 did not gel. This is because the protease in the pineapple broke down the protein in the gelatin preventing it from gelling. The gelatin in cups 2 and 3 should have gelled or at least gotten very thick compared to cup 1. This is because the acid in cup 2 and the heat applied to the pineapple juice in cup 3 damaged the protease preventing it from breaking down the protein in the gelatin. Why do you think we needed cup 4? Whenever you do an experiment, you need a control. This is the item that you compare all of the other tests against. This shows what happens if you do not do anything. Cup 4 is a regular cup of gelatin. You can then compare each of the cups to cup 4 to see what happens when you make one change at a time.

Biochemistry

Decomposers

Ultimate recycling

What is the nitrogen cycle?

Words to know:

decomposition   decomposer

scavenger

Have you ever thought about what happens to a plant after it stops growing and withers? Have you ever seen a dead animal beside the road and wondered what would become of it? God has provided a way for the chemicals in dead plants and animals to be recycled. This process of recycling is called **decomposition.**

One of the most important elements that is recycled is nitrogen. Nitrogen is necessary for plant growth, and plants absorb nitrogen from the soil. Some of this nitrogen is then absorbed into an animal's body when the animal eats the plant. If another animal later eats that animal, the nitrogen passes on to the larger animal's body. Once the animal dies, it then decays and the nitrogen is returned to the soil.

Consider what would happen if plants and animals did not decay. The nitrogen in their bodies would be "lost" because it could not be reused, and eventually the earth would run out of nitrogen and new plants could no longer grow. Instead, there are special organisms to help break down dead plants and animals so that the nitrogen and other chemicals can be reused.

Scavengers are the first animals that help in the decomposition process. Scavengers are animals that eat dead animals. One common scavenger is the vulture. Lions, bears, jackals, hyenas, and komodo dragons are also scavengers. Sea sponges and insects are scavengers as well. Once the scavenger has eaten the dead animal, some of the chemicals become part of its body, but many of the chemicals are eliminated through its dung.

Organisms called **decomposers** then break down the nitrogen compounds and other complex chemicals in the animal waste into simple compounds.

Scavengers are the first animals that help in the decomposition process.

Biochemistry

🧪 The nitrogen cycle

Purpose: To draw a picture of the nitrogen cycle

Materials: drawing paper, colored pencils

Procedure:

1. Draw a picture of a plant in the center of the page, showing that nitrogen is being absorbed from the ground by the plant's roots.

2. Draw an arrow to a small animal, such as a mouse, that eats the plant.

3. Draw an arrow to a larger animal, perhaps an eagle or an owl, that eats the smaller animal.

4. The next arrow should point from the large animal to a scavenger, such as a vulture.

5. From the vulture there should be an arrow to dung on the ground. This picture needs to be labeled as having bacteria.

6. The final arrow should point to the plant, showing that the nitrogen has completed the cycle and is ready to be absorbed by a plant again.

7. Label the picture with the words "Nitrogen Cycle."

Conclusion: This picture demonstrates the path that nitrogen takes as it is used to support life on earth. Be sure to note that people absorb nitrogen when they eat plants as well. The nitrogen cycle is God's plan for recycling nitrogen. In addition to nitrogen, other chemicals are recycled in a similar manner. Recall the carbon cycle you learned about in lesson 9.

The nitrogen cycle is actually much more complex than we have explained in the lesson. Nitrogen is recycled in several different ways. Interestingly, lightning also plays a role in the nitrogen cycle by moving nitrogen from the air into the soil.

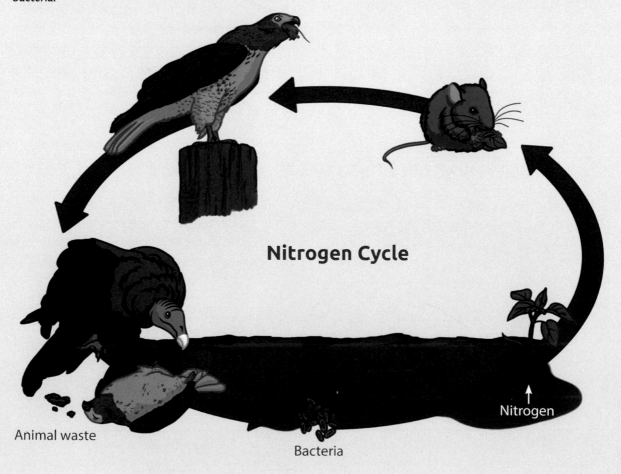

Nitrogen Cycle

Animal waste

Bacteria

Nitrogen

Mold is a fungus that can grow quickly on bread.

These decomposers are simple organisms like bacteria and fungi. Decomposers also work directly on dead animals and plants to break them down into elements that can be reused by plants growing nearby.

God created the first man, Adam, from the dust of the ground to live forever (Genesis 1:27). Adam's sin brought death into the world (Romans 5:12) as part of God's curse on the world. Now when animals or people die, their bodies return to the dust of the ground (Genesis 3:19) and are recycled, like plants. God has even designed the effects of man's sin to be a blessing to the earth through the nitrogen cycle. ✳

What did we learn?

- What is a scavenger?
- What is a decomposer?
- What is this way of recycling nitrogen called?

Taking it further

- Why are decomposers necessary?
- Were there animal scavengers in God's perfect creation, before the Fall of man?
- Explain how a compost pile allows you to participate in the nitrogen cycle.

Rate of decomposition

The most common decomposers are microscopic bacteria and fungi. These organisms are found on nearly every surface in the world. You can't get away from them even if you wanted to, but you can control and affect the rate at which decomposers work. Think about mold growing on your food. What conditions seem to encourage mold growth? What conditions seem to discourage it? You can test the effects of various conditions on decomposers by completing the following experiment in which yeast, which is a fungus, will be used to aid in the decomposition of a banana.

Purpose: To test the effects of various conditions on the rate of decomposition

Materials: three plastic zipper bags, banana, baking yeast, "Rate of Decomposition" worksheet

Procedure:

1. Label three plastic zipper bags with the conditions in which you will be testing decomposition:
   - Cold and dark
   - Warm and dark
   - Warm and light

2. Peel a banana and divide it into three equal pieces. Place one piece in each bag.

3. Sprinkle ½ teaspoon of baking yeast over each banana piece then seal each bag.

4. Place the bag testing cold and dark conditions in a location in a refrigerator where it will not be disturbed.

5. Place the bag testing warm and dark conditions in a cupboard where it will not be disturbed.

6. Place the bag testing warm and light conditions in a sunny location where it will not be disturbed.

7. Predict which bag you expect to see the fastest decomposition in. Write your hypothesis on the "Rate of Decomposition" worksheet.

8. Observe each bag daily for one week. Write your observations on your worksheet. Be sure to include how the banana looks, how the bag looks, how the banana feels, and any smells that you observe.

9. At the end of one week, compare your observations with your hypothesis and see if you were right.

Biochemistry

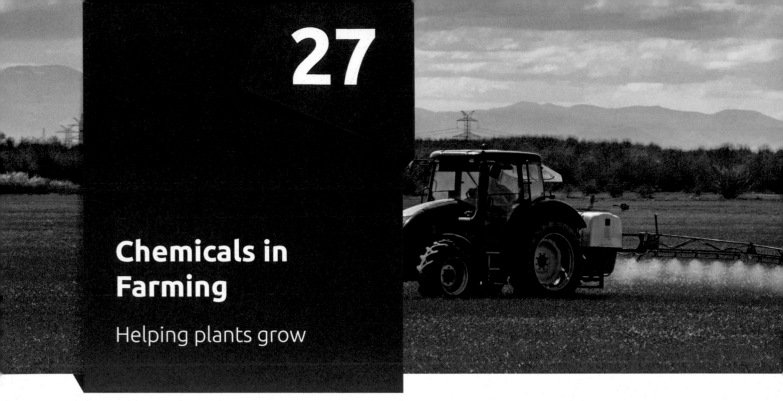

Chemicals in Farming

Helping plants grow

How do farmers use chemicals?

Words to know:

crop rotation	fungicide
fallow	herbicide
fertilizer	organic farming
hydroponics	genetic engineering
pesticide	genetic modification

As you learned in the last lesson, decomposers help nitrogen and other elements return to the soil to be reused by plants. This system works very well in natural areas. However, continuous farming of a piece of land uses up the nutrients, particularly nitrogen, faster than decomposers can replace them. In order to maintain healthy usable soil, the nutrients must be replaced.

There are several methods for replacing the nutrients in the soil. One of the oldest methods of keeping the soil viable is to use **crop rotation**. Different crops use nutrients in different amounts, and some crops, such as beans and alfalfa, actually return nitrogen to the soil, so planting different crops from year to year helps to keep the soil useful. Also, allowing a portion of the land to lie **fallow**, without crops,

allows the bacteria in the soil to have enough time to return the needed nitrogen.

Crop rotation has been used for centuries. In the nineteenth century, parts of Europe, and England in particular, followed the Norfolk 4-course crop rotation plan. In the first year, the farmer would plant a root crop such as turnips. Year two, he would plant barley. Year three, he would plant grass or clover and allow animals to graze on it. Then, in the fourth year, he would plant wheat. Farmers repeated this cycle, and it helped to keep their land productive.

A second method for adding nutrients back to the soil is through fertilization. Nitrogen,

Nitrogen, phosphorous, and other chemicals can be added to the soil with man-made fertilizers.

Biochemistry

phosphorous, and other chemicals can be added to the soil in one of two ways. One way is through the application of animal dung. Much of the nitrogen that is in the plants that animals eat comes out through the animal's waste. So, applying animal waste to the land is one way to improve the soil's productivity. A second way to add nutrients back to the soil is to add artificial or man-made **fertilizers**. These are chemicals that are prepared in a laboratory or factory and then applied to the soil.

The third method of improving the soil is through burning. This method is used primarily in tropical areas where plant growth is rapid. Much of the nitrogen and other chemicals become tied up in unwanted plants that grow in the fields. Farmers burn these plants, and the ash returns the chemicals to the soil. Then the fields can be planted with desired crops.

Chemistry is important to farming in many ways other than just the nutrients in the soil. In fact, one type of farming does not use soil at all. **Hydroponics** is a type of farming in which plants are attached to some sort of supporting framework and the roots are bathed in a water solution containing boron, calcium, nitrogen, phosphorous, potassium, and other chemicals. Hydroponics was first used on a large scale by U.S. troops in the Pacific Islands during World War II. Canada began selling hydroponic tomatoes to

A crop of organic hydroponic tomatoes

consumers in 1988. Today, it is often more economical to grow many flowers and vegetables using hydroponics than in the traditional manner.

In addition to the chemicals needed by the plants, farmers also use chemicals as pesticides, fungicides, and herbicides. **Pesticides** are chemicals that are used to control insects and other pests that might damage crops. **Fungicides** are chemicals that kill fungi, which often cause diseases in plants. **Herbicides** are chemicals that kill unwanted plants, like weeds, without damaging the desired crops. Researchers are always trying to find better chemicals to help crops grow without leaving behind chemicals that will hurt the consumer.

🧪 The effects of fertilizer

Purpose: To demonstrate the effect of fertilizer on plants

Materials: two identical plants, plant food

Procedure:

1. Obtain two identical plants. Label one plant as plant A and the other as plant B.

2. Prepare a solution of water and plant food according to the manufacturer's directions. Save this solution to use each day to water one of the plants.

3. Pour ¼ cup of water without plant food on the soil of plant A each day. Pour ¼ cup of the water and plant food solution on the soil of plant B each day. If ¼ cup is too much or too little water to keep the soil moist but not soggy, adjust the amount as needed. However, be

sure that both plants are receiving the same amount of liquid each time.

Questions: Based on what you have learned, which plant would you expect to grow faster? Why?

Conclusion: After a few days it should become obvious that the plant receiving the plant food is growing better than the plant without it. This is because the additional chemicals in the plant food provide the necessary nutrients for plant growth. If you did not see a significant difference, why do you think the plant growth was the same? (If the soil already had as much nutrients as the plants could use, adding more nutrients would not increase its growth. You can transplant both plants into less productive soil and try the experiment again.)

Biochemistry

Because many people have concerns about eating crops that are treated with chemicals, some farmers have gone organic. Those who follow organic farming methods grow their crops without the use of any artificial chemicals. These crops are often more expensive because the organic farmer has to deal with insects and weeds more than other farmers do. But many people feel that organic produce is a healthier choice. You and your family will have to decide for yourselves.

Genetic engineering is another method that scientists are developing to help avoid the use of so many chemicals. Many crops have been modified with genes that make them resistant to certain diseases or undesirable to certain pests. Genetic modification can also make some crop plants more resistant to herbicides so only the weeds will be killed, but the plant will not be harmed. A large percentage of produce in our supermarkets is genetically modified in some way. ✳

What did we learn?

- What are three ways that farmers ensure their soil will have enough nutrients for their crops?

- What is hydroponics?

- How are chemicals used in farming other than for nutrients for the plants?

- How is an organic farm different from other farms?

Taking it further

- Why did the farmers let cattle graze on their land once every fourth year in the Norfolk 4-course plant rotation method?

- How does hydroponics replace the role of soil in plant growth?

Organic farming

Organic farming has become more popular in recent decades. Organic farmers reject the use of artificial chemicals as well as genetically modified organisms. They claim to use more natural ways to control weeds and insects. There is much controversy and little agreement about the advantages and disadvantages of organic farming. See what you can find out about the pros and cons on each of the following aspects of organic farming:

1. Controlling pests—are organic methods effective?

2. Productivity—which way produces more crops?

3. Labor required—which way requires more labor?

4. Genetically modified organisms—are they good or bad?

5. The environment—which farming method is friendlier to the environment?

6. Food quality—which is better?

7. Food health—which is healthier?

There are many other issues and controversies surrounding organic farming and the use of chemicals, but starting with these questions will give you a good introduction to organic farming. Try to find out the arguments on both sides of each issue. Share what you learn with your class or family.

Biochemistry

28

Medicines

Chemical compounds that affect your body

How do chemical compounds help heal your body?

Words to know:

pharmaceutical	synthetic
medicine	antibiotic
herb	vaccine
anesthetic	ethnobotanist

Challenge words:

chemotherapy

Your body is a living chemistry lab. We have already discussed some of the chemical processes involved in your body, such as breathing and digestion. Because your body works with chemicals, adding different chemical compounds to your body can greatly affect how you feel and how your body responds. For this reason, you need to be very careful what chemicals you allow into your body. Some chemicals can be very harmful and others can be very helpful. Some helpful chemicals are **pharmaceuticals** or **medicines**.

Herbs were the first plants to be used for healing purposes. From after the Fall until today, people have used various plants as cures for different illnesses. Some have been more effective than others, but many have been very effective even if the user did not know why. Most herbal remedies were discovered by trial and error.

The bark of certain trees has been used to cure headaches. This remedy has been found in the records of the Egyptians, the Chinese, and the Sumerians, as much as 3,000 years ago. But it wasn't until the nineteenth century that scientists discovered that the tree bark contained salicylic acid, which today is the main ingredient in aspirin. The Bayer Company began selling aspirin as a medication in 1899.

The different effects of chemical compounds began to be studied in earnest in the nineteenth century, and since then many helpful discoveries have been made. In 1799 Sir Humphry Davy discovered that nitrous oxide could be used as an **anesthetic** to stop pain. Today we know this chemical as laughing gas, and it is frequently used in dental offices to eliminate the pain of dental procedures. In 1831

Fun Fact

Americans spend $5 billion each year on medicines that are derived from plants.

chloroform was discovered, and in 1842 ether was used during an operation for the first time. These and other anesthetic chemicals make it possible for doctors to perform operations without their patients feeling pain during the procedure.

When a patient takes a painkiller such as aspirin, or receives an anesthetic, the chemical in the medication locks onto the nerve cells in the brain. This prevents the pain signals from getting through, so the patient does not feel the pain. This process is like a chemical lock and key. The chemical is a key to locking up your pain receptors.

Shortly after these discoveries, many other drugs were discovered. The first **synthetic**, or man-made, drug was developed in 1910. Then, in 1930, a group of drugs called sulpha drugs was developed to kill some bacteria. But the really big break in medicine came in 1928 with the discovery of penicillin by Sir Alexander Fleming. The process for mass producing penicillin was discovered by Andrew Moyer. Penicillin was the first antibiotic. An **antibiotic** is a substance produced by living organisms that is used to kill bacteria. Since the 1940s, dozens of other antibiotics have been discovered, such as amoxicillin and tetracycline.

Andrew Moyer discovered the process for mass producing penicillin.

In addition to antibiotics, another important medical use of chemicals is vaccinations. **Vaccines** are chemical solutions that have been developed to help stimulate your body's natural defenses against certain diseases. This helps to keep you from developing those diseases. Edward Jenner tested the first vaccine in 1796 when he gave an injection containing cowpox to people to help them develop immunity to smallpox.

The search for new medicines continues. A person who studies plants in order to develop new medicines is called an **ethnobotanist**. These scientists try to find plants with chemical compounds that are beneficial to the human body. Only about 0.5% of all plants in the world today have been tested for medicinal purposes. There may be many helpful substances that God has placed in the

Fun Fact

Genetic engineers are working on developing new organisms that can quickly produce needed chemicals for medications.

Common herbs

Man has used herbal remedies for centuries. Ginger is commonly used to settle an upset stomach. Certain oils have been used to improve digestion. Garlic is a natural antibiotic and has been shown to help lower cholesterol. Ginseng is an herb that increases your energy level. The list goes on and on. You can enjoy the benefits of some of these natural herbal substances by making a fun snack of garlic bread and ginger ale.

Spread butter or margarine on a piece of bread. Sprinkle a small amount of garlic powder on the bread. Toast under the broiler of your oven until golden. Enjoy this natural antibiotic with a cool glass of ginger ale.

Ginger root   Garlic

Biochemistry

world just waiting to be discovered and used to benefit mankind. ✳

 # What did we learn?

- Why are chemicals used as medicines?
- What were the earliest recorded medicines?
- What was Sir Alexander Fleming's important discovery?

 # Taking it further

- If plants have the potential of supplying new medicines, where might a person look to find different plants?
- What other sources might there be for discovering new medicines?

Chemotherapy

Chemicals have been used to treat various kinds of cancer since the 1950s. This type of treatment is called **chemotherapy**. Chemotherapy originally meant any kind of chemical used to treat a disease, but today it specifically applies to chemicals used to treat cancer.

There are many different kinds of cancer, but all cancers are diseases that involve cells that are growing and reproducing out of control. Drugs that treat cancer have been developed to target cells that are reproducing very quickly. Cells in your body can be in one of several states with respect to reproduction. The cells can be resting, meaning they are performing their designed functions, they can be preparing to reproduce, or they can be in the process of reproducing. Noncancerous cells spend much of their time in the resting phase; however, cancer cells spend a large part of their time preparing to reproduce or actually reproducing. Therefore, chemotherapy drugs have been designed to target cells that are either preparing to reproduce or actually reproducing.

These drugs chemically interact with reproducing cells to prevent them from completing the reproduction cycle, and destroy the cells. This can be very effective in eliminating cancer cells. However, the drugs cannot distinguish cancer cells from noncancer cells; they only react with reproducing cells and leave resting cells alone. Thus, other cells in the body that reproduce quickly are more affected by the chemotherapy than slowly reproducing cells.

Hair cells reproduce very quickly and are often destroyed by the chemicals used in chemotherapy. This is why many cancer patients lose their hair during treatment. Also, the cells in the lining of the stomach

Hair cells reproduce very quickly and are often destroyed by the chemicals used in chemotherapy.

and intestines are replaced very quickly, so these cells are also harmed by the chemotherapy, often resulting in upset stomach and vomiting.

Overall, doctors must balance the use of the chemicals to destroy the cancer cells with the amount of side effects the patient can withstand. Decades of testing and treatment have resulted in very effective uses of chemicals to treat many forms of cancer.

Chemicals administered by doctors are not the only treatments that people use for cancer. Some people have had success in using herbs and special diets to change the chemical balance in their bodies and thus slow down or eliminate some cancers. Our bodies are very complex, and chemicals have drastic effects on many functions. Therefore, we must be careful what chemicals we put into our bodies. On the other hand, God has miraculously designed our bodies to heal themselves in many ways, by fighting disease and rebuilding damaged tissues. So we can see the hand of God in our bodies every day.

Alexander Fleming is a name you may not know, but you can be thankful for what he did. He discovered penicillin, a medicine made from a mold that kills harmful bacteria. Who was this man that would try such a thing? Alexander Fleming was born in Scotland in 1881, the seventh of eight children. The family worked an 800-acre farm where the children spent much of their time roaming the countryside. Later in life Alexander said, "We unconsciously learned a great deal from nature."

His father passed away when Alexander was 14. His oldest brother took over the farm, and Alec, as he was called, along with four of his siblings left Scotland and moved to London. After completing his schooling, Alec went to work for a shipping company, but he did not like it very much. So when the Boer War in South Africa broke out in 1900, Alexander and two of his brothers joined a Scottish regiment. This unit was never sent to war but spent most of its time playing different sports, such as shooting, swimming, and water polo.

It was around this time that Alec's uncle died and left an inheritance of about 250 British pounds to each of the Fleming children. Tom, Alec's brother, encouraged him to use his inheritance to study medicine. Alexander made top scores on the entrance exam and won a scholarship to St. Mary's, the school he preferred because he had played water polo against them. After completing his training, he could have left St. Mary's and taken a position as a surgeon. However, the captain of St. Mary's rifle club wanted Alec to stay and be part of his rifle team, so he encouraged Alec to switch from surgery to bacteriology, which he did.

In 1915 Alexander married an Irish woman named Sarah Marion, and they had a son who became a physician. When World War I started, Alec, and most of the people who worked in the lab he

was in, went to France and set up a battlefield hospital lab. There on the battlefield he saw firsthand how small wounds could become infected and often lead to death. He felt that there must be some chemical solution that could help prevent this. He made many innovations in the treatment of the wounded during the war that helped decrease the mortality rate, but he had yet to discover something that would prevent infection.

After the war, Fleming spent most of his time researching different chemicals and made some important discoveries, but none as important as what he found in 1928. Fleming had been growing mold and bacteria in several different petri dishes. He had stacked several of them in the sink and did not get around to cleaning them up right away. When he finally did get around to cleaning up his

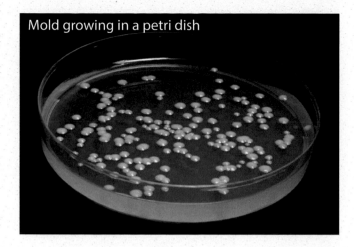

Mold growing in a petri dish

experiments, he looked at each one before putting it into the cleaning solution. One dish made him stop and say, "That's funny." In this dish, some mold had grown, and around the mold the staph bacteria had died. He sampled the mold and found it to belong to the penicillium family. He labeled his discovery penicillin.

He published his findings in 1929, but it raised little interest. Fleming found it difficult to process the penicillin and a group of chemists took over the work for him. Eventually, even this work stopped when several of the chemists either died or moved away. Fleming's work on penicillin did not advance

much more until World War II started. At that time, Howard Florey and Ernst Chain started up the work again.

They were able to demonstrate how effective penicillin is against several infectious diseases and described the mechanisms for how it works. For this work Florey, Chain, and Fleming shared the 1945 Nobel Prize for Chemistry.

However, they were still unable to produce enough penicillin for commercial use. And with World War II still raging, it was important to find a way to produce it so that soldiers could be treated in the battlefield and not die from infections. So in 1941, Florey went to the United States and worked with Andrew Moyer. Together they developed a method for mass producing penicillin. In 1940 penicillin was so rare it was nearly priceless. In 1943 it was $20 per dose, and by 1946 it was only $0.55 per dose. All of these men were responsible for discovering a way to save millions of lives.

In 1944 Fleming was knighted for his discovery of penicillin. In 1947 Dr. Fleming became the director of the Wright-Fleming Institute of St. Mary's Hospital. He died in 1955 at the age of 73, and his body now rests in St. Paul's Cathedral in London.

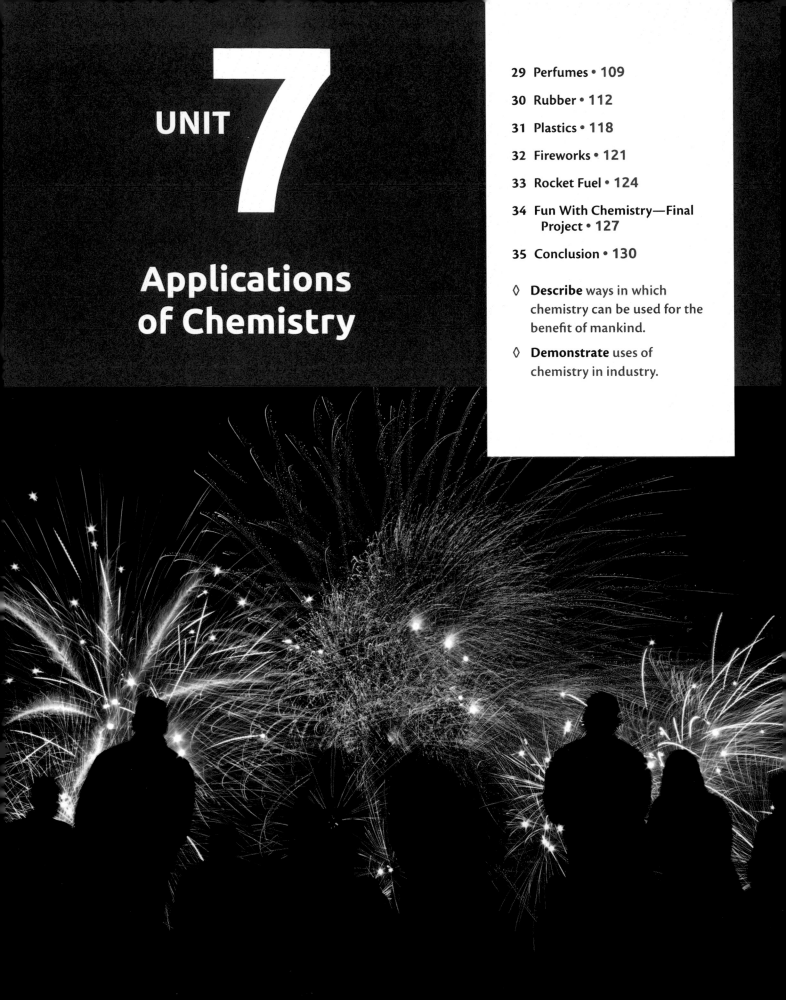

UNIT 7

Applications of Chemistry

◊ **Describe** ways in which chemistry can be used for the benefit of mankind.

◊ **Demonstrate** uses of chemistry in industry.

29

Perfumes

What's that smell?

How are the scents in perfumes made?

Words to know:

perfume

aromatic

solvent extraction

steam distillation

Have you ever walked through a depart-ment store and smelled the perfumes near the cosmetic area? You may have liked some scents and disliked others. Perfumes and colognes are very popular with many people. But you probably never realized that chemistry plays an important role in making these scents. In the next several lessons, we will be learning about many different ways that chemistry is used in the world around us, and we will begin with a look at perfume.

A **perfume** is a liquid with a pleasant smell. It is **aromatic**; this means that its smell is easily detected by the human nose. In order for the liquid to be aromatic, it must contain scent molecules that are light enough to float in the air so they will reach the nose. Molecules that are water soluble or fat/oil soluble are the most aromatic.

Most perfumes are made by extracting scent molecules from plants that are considered to have a pleasant smell. Flowers are the most common source of scent molecules used in the making of perfumes. And this is where an understanding of chemistry becomes important.

The scent of a flower petal comes from the oil in the petals and this oil must be removed in order to make the perfume. There are two main methods for extracting these scent molecules from plants. The first is called **solvent extraction**. In this method, the flower petals are soaked in a solvent. The solvent is a chemical in which the oil containing the scent will dissolve. The flower parts are then removed. Next, the solvent is allowed to evaporate. This leaves the fragrant oil behind.

Steam distillation aparatus

The second method of scent extraction is called **steam distillation**. In this method, steam is passed through the petals causing the oil to vaporize. The oil moves with the steam through a tube to another container where both the oil and water condense and become liquids. The water sinks to the bottom of the container and the oil floats on the top of the water. The oil is then skimmed off the water and removed.

Once the fragrant oil is obtained, the perfume is made by combining the oil with an alcohol. This is done so that the oil is easily sprayed onto your skin. The alcohol quickly evaporates, leaving behind the desired fragrance.

What did we learn?

- What is a perfume?
- What must be removed from flower petals to make perfume?
- Describe the two main methods for removing oil from flower petals.

Taking it further

- Why should you test a new perfume on your skin before you buy it?
- Why wasn't it necessary to use one of the methods described in the lesson to make your homemade perfume?

Making your own perfume

You can easily make your own perfume. Many of you performing this experiment are probably thinking, "I'm a guy, and guys don't wear perfume." Well this may be true, but many men wear cologne, which is a scent designed for a man. So you can make cologne instead of perfume. You will be using cloves, which is a scent that is not particularly feminine or masculine.

Purpose: To make your own perfume/cologne

Materials: cloves, jar with lid, rubbing alcohol

Procedure:

1. Place 15 whole cloves in the bottom of a jar.
2. Add ¼ cup of rubbing alcohol to the jar and close the lid.
3. Allow this solution to sit for seven days.
4. At the end of one week, remove the cloves from the alcohol and you have your own perfume.

Conclusion: The perfume may not smell like cloves when you sniff the jar, but take a small amount of the liquid and place it on your skin. The alcohol quickly evaporates, leaving behind a pleasant clove scent.

🏅 Scents

If you have ever been to a department store, you will find that there are hundreds of different scents available for perfumes and colognes. This is because the same scent may not smell the same on two different people. Not only do scent molecules evaporate from your skin, but they can chemically combine with the oils on your skin to produce a different scent. So the scent you like so much on your best friend might smell terrible on you.

Also, each person's nose is sensitive to different scents. Although you may love the smell of coffee, another person might hate it. So a whole industry has developed producing hundreds of different scents for people to wear.

The scents in perfume are actually much more complex than just a single scent like the clove perfume you made. Most perfumes contain several scents combined together. Often a perfume will be made of at least three scents. The first scent that you smell is called the head. This is usually a strong scent that is easily detected but easily evaporates and lasts for only a short period of time. Orange is a common head scent. The second scent is called the heart. This is usually a floral scent and is the smell you most associate with the perfume. The final scent is called the base. This is the smell that lasts the longest and is usually more subtle than the other scents. Common bases include sandalwood and vanilla. The combination of smells results in a pleasant experience. You immediately smell the head scent, but then the smell melts into a combination of the heart and base scents, slowly changing over time.

You can try to produce your own personalized perfume or cologne. Try soaking different items in alcohol for several days to make a scent you really like. You can choose from the following list, or come up with your own ideas. Try several scents and see which ones you like best.

- ginger root
- mint leaves
- cinnamon sticks
- dried fruit
- different flowers
- allspice

Some cooking extracts may make pleasant perfumes or colognes. You might consider:

- peppermint oil
- almond extract
- vanilla extract

Today many households have essential oils on hand. Essential oils are oils that have been extracted from plants, usually by distillation just like we described in the lesson. Many of these oils are safe to use on the skin. If you have essential oils that are safe for the skin, you could combine small amounts of two or three oils to make a perfume as well.

30

Rubber

Do you have a rubber band?

How is rubber made, and what is it used for?

Words to know:

rubber   vulcanization

latex   polymer

Challenge words:

rosin   casein

lac   keratin

silk

You place it on the end of your finger and slowly stretch it back; then suddenly you release it and it goes flying across the room! Who hasn't experienced the thrill of launching a rubber band? It's great fun to try to improve your aim and hit a target. (Just don't hit your brother or sister!) But did you know that there is a lot of chemistry involved in making a rubber band?

Rubber is made from a naturally occurring substance called latex. **Latex** is a sticky, milky-colored material that is found in rubber trees. Rubber products became very popular in the early 1800s.

However, two major problems occurred with the original rubber products. First, when the rubber got cold, like during a winter storm, it became brittle and cracked. Second, when the rubber got very warm, like in the middle of summer, it became sticky. Rubber products were not very useful if they could only be used in mild temperatures. A car with rubber tires wasn't very useful if you could only drive it in the spring and the fall.

So scientists worked very hard to find a way to make rubber more useful. In 1839 a chemist named Charles Goodyear discovered how to improve

Tapping latex from a rubber tree

rubber's performance. He found that adding sulfur to the latex caused it to become elastic and eliminated the bad reactions to extreme temperatures. This process is called **vulcanization**.

Rubber is a chemical that forms long chains of carbon and hydrogen molecules into what are called **polymers**. These linked molecules can pivot around the carbon atoms, allowing rubber to change it shape. Naturally, these long chains of molecules are a random mess. But when an outside force is added, the chains can be stretched out and become parallel to each other. The chemical attraction of the covalent bonds pulls the molecules back into their original shape when the outside force is gone. Vulcanized rubber adds sulfur atoms to the polymer chains, connecting them together so that they act like one big molecule. This helps the rubber retain its elasticity, even at extreme temperatures.

Once vulcanization was discovered, rubber became very popular. People began trying to make nearly everything out of rubber. Of course, one of the most important uses for rubber was automobile tires, but clothing, shoes, balls, grommets, erasers, and many other items were made of rubber as well.

This dependence on rubber became a real problem during World War II. After attacking Asia, Japan controlled most of the rubber tree plantations there,

Fun Fact

Synthetic rubber became widespread after World War II. In 1960 the use of synthetic rubber surpassed the use of natural rubber and this trend continues today.

and the Axis powers together controlled nearly 95% of all natural rubber supplies. This created a crisis for America. To make a Sherman tank required ½ ton of rubber, not to mention all of the other rubber products required to keep an army functioning. So America did two things. First, the whole country did a major recycling campaign to provide enough rubber to keep the army going for at least a year or two. And second, the president asked scientists to develop an economical synthetic rubber.

Synthetic rubber had been discovered in 1875, but it was too expensive to make so it had not been developed. During World War II it became crucial for the United States to find an inexpensive synthetic rubber, and that is exactly what the scientists did. The process they discovered is still used today. First, scientists extract a chemical called naphtha from petroleum. Naphtha is then sent through a chemical process to change it into polymers that

Many everyday objects are made from rubber.

are very similar to natural rubber. This discovery helped America win the war and led to a boom in the number of uses for both natural and synthetic rubber.

Today, a large percentage of the rubber used around the world is produced from petroleum instead of latex from rubber trees. Synthetic and natural rubber are used in everything from cars to bikes, and from running shoes to clothing. Whether the rubber is natural or man-made, it is still fun to shoot a rubber band. ✳

What did we learn?

- What is natural rubber made from?
- What is synthetic rubber made from?
- What is vulcanization?
- What is a polymer?

Taking it further

- Why is it difficult to recycle automobile tires?
- What advantages and disadvantages are there to using synthetic rubber instead of natural rubber?

Fun Fact

In 1943 James Wright was trying to produce a synthetic rubber, but only succeeded in producing a thick putty-like material. He put it on the shelf and forgot about it. A few years later a salesman picked it up and used it to entertain some customers. The value of the putty as a toy was soon recognized and in 1957 it was introduced to the world as Silly Putty.

Playing with rubber

Purpose: To understand how rubber polymers act

Materials: latex balloon, marker, wide rubber band

Activity 1—Procedure:

1. Inflate a balloon, but do not tie it closed.

2. While you hold the inflated balloon, draw a picture or write a message on the balloon (you may need someone to help with this step).

3. Let the air out of the balloon and look at the picture. Has it changed?

Conclusion: Most balloons are made from latex. This latex may be natural or synthetic, but it has the same effect. The polymer fibers of the balloon are all coiled up when it is deflated. As you inflate the balloon, the fibers are forced to stretch out and become straight. After you released the air the stretched molecules returned to their original shape, and the picture has shrunk and changed shape along with it.

Activity 2—Procedure:

1. Stretch a wide rubber band and quickly place it against your forehead. How does it feel? (It should feel warm.)

2. Remove the rubber band from your forehead and release the pressure on the rubber band, then quickly place it against your forehead again. How does it feel now? (It should feel cool.)

Conclusion: The polymers release energy when they are stretched out so the rubber band feels warm for a few seconds after it is stretched out. The polymers gain energy when they recoil, so the rubber band feels cool for a few seconds after it returns to its normal shape.

🏅 Polymers

Latex is the natural polymer from which rubber is made, but latex is not the only natural polymer. Many other products are made from natural polymers as well. Dead wood and wood pulp contain a polymer called **rosin**. Rosin is used to make varnish and soap. It is also used by violinists to keep their bows smooth and by gymnasts who want to keep their grip on the equipment.

Animals also produce polymers that are useful. An insect called the lac (*Kerria lacca*) produces a polymer that is also called **lac**. Lac is used to make lacquer, which is used as a shiny coating on furniture and other surfaces. Silkworms produce **silk** which is also a polymer. The strands of a silkworm cocoon are unwound and woven into soft beautiful cloth. This natural polymer was one of the most important trade items between Europe and Asia for many centuries.

Cattle also produce a couple of polymers that are very important. Cow's milk contains a protein called **casein**. This natural polymer is used in making cheese as well as in making artificial gems. Its long molecules work as a glue to hold cheese together and to hold together the ingredients for artificial gems.

Finally, horns of several animals contain **keratin**.

Cow's milk contains casein.

Your body also contains keratin. You find it in your hair and fingernails as well as in your skin cells. This polymer keeps your body watertight. There are many other natural polymers. If you find this interesting, you can do more exploration and find out more information about natural polymers such as cellulose and amber.

Silkworm cocoon

A rhino's horns contain keratin.

Charles Goodyear

1800–1860

The use of rubber is not new. The Indians of Central and South America were using it for centuries before Columbus found it and introduced it to western culture. The Indians called it *caoutchouc* from the word *cahuchu* which means *weeping tree*. But the Europeans called it *rubber* because it could be used to rub out pencil marks, what today we would call an eraser. However, rubber did not have many uses until after 1839 because it had two main problems. In the heat of the summer it turned into a gooey mess, and in the winter it became stiff and brittle. In 1839 this all changed, possibly by accident, but certainly through hard work.

Nine years earlier, Charles Goodyear, a bankrupt hardware merchant, walked into the Roxbury India Rubber Company in New York to sell them a new valve, but this company was about to go bankrupt. The problem was that summer had come and all the products they had been selling were being returned because the rubber was melting. The directors, in an effort to keep things quiet, had even met in the middle of the night to bury $20,000 worth of the melting products in a pit. So Goodyear was unable to sell his valve. But after hearing this, Charles, at the age of 34, decided to take his first good look at rubber to try and understand how it worked.

Since his trip was unsuccessful, he returned to Philadelphia and was put in jail for not paying his debts. While in jail, he put his time to good use. He had his wife bring him some raw rubber and a rolling pin, and he did his first experiments with the gummy mess.

He tried adding drying powders like magnesia to the rubber with some promising results. Once out of jail, Charles, his wife, and their daughters made up hundreds of pairs of magnesia-dried rubber overshoes in their kitchen. Unfortunately, the heat of summer came before he could sell them and the

overshoes turned into a shapeless paste. And the Goodyears were again penniless.

Because his neighbors complained about Goodyear's smelly work, he felt compelled to move. So he moved to New York. There, Goodyear tried adding two drying agents, magnesia and quicklime, to the rubber. He was getting much better results, well enough that he received a medal at a New York trade show.

A further advancement came by accident. Charles put designs on the products he sold. And one time he used nitric acid to remove his design and found that it turned the rubber black. He threw this piece away only to retrieve it later because he remembered it also made the rubber smooth and dry. It was a better rubber than anyone had ever made. A businessman advanced him several thousand dollars to start producing this rubber. However, the 1837 financial panic wiped out the business and Charles and his family again lost everything. They ended up camping in an abandoned rubber factory on Staten Island and eating the fish they caught. But Goodyear did not give up.

Eventually, Goodyear moved to Boston and got financial backing to make mailbags for the government using his nitric acid rubber. He made 150 bags and left them in a warm storeroom while he took his family on a month-long vacation. When he returned he found that the mailbags had melted and were useless.

Goodyear again hit rock bottom and was dependent on the kindness of farmers to give his children milk and half-grown potatoes to survive. Next, he started using sulfur in his work with rubber. The details of how he made his famous discovery are not clear or consistent, but the most reliable story says that one cold day in February he went into the general store in Woburn, Massachusetts to show off his latest gum-and-sulfur rubber when the customers sitting around the cracker-barrel started snickering at him. He must have been on very hard times because he was normally a mild-mannered man, but this day he got excited and started waving a fistful of his gummy substance in the air. It flew out of his hand and landed on a hot stove and proceeded to cook. He went over to scrape it off the surface, thinking it would melt like molasses. Instead, what he found was a leathery rubber that had elasticity. This rubber was remarkably different from the other rubbers he had tried before; it was a weatherproof rubber. Goodyear denied this incident and said his discovery was not an accident.

That winter took its toll on Charles and his family. Due to failing health, he hobbled around doing his experiments on crutches. But he now knew that heat and sulfur held the answer he was looking for. The questions remained: how much sulfur, what temperature, and how long to heat it? After extensive experimentation, Goodyear at last found the right combination of sulfur, heat, and time. He found that pressurized steam at 270°F (132°C) for four to six hours gave the best results. This process is now called vulcanization.

Charles evidently wrote his wealthy brother-in-law about his discovery and his bother-in-law took an immediate interest in using the rubber as a textile. Two factories were put into production as the new form of rubber became a worldwide success. Unfortunately, Goodyear disposed of his manufacturing interest as soon as he could, and he never saw the millions he might have made.

Charles Goodyear was a good inventor, but not a good businessman. For instance, the people holding rights to his rubber made $3.00 a yard on the rubber they sold, while Mr. Goodyear made only 3 cents per yard. He was also in 32 different patent infringement cases. Some court cases went as high as the U.S. Supreme Court. In one of the cases, Goodyear hired Daniel Webster, at that time the Secretary of State, and paid him $15,000 to temporarily step down from office and work as his lawyer. This was the largest sum paid to a lawyer at that time. Mr. Webster's two-day speech won a permanent injunction against further patent infringements in the U.S., securing some rights for Goodyear. In spite of this victory however, Charles died in 1860, $200,000 in debt.

Goodyear's family did eventually recover some of the royalties due them and eventually made a comfortable living. They finally reaped the reward for their father's undying commitment to the production of rubber. Today, we can't imagine life without rubber tires, rubber boots and shoes, rubber seals, and a host of other rubber products; all because Charles Goodyear did not give up.

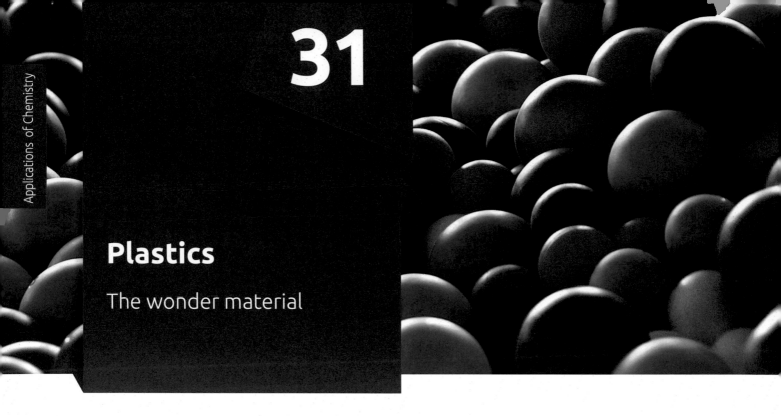

31

Plastics

The wonder material

How are plastics made, and what are they used for?

Words to know:

plastic

thermoplastic

thermosetting resin

What would your life be like without plastic? Look around your home and notice how many items are made from plastic. Your mixer or blender, the handle on your refrigerator, buttons, light switch covers, even your clothes are probably made from some kind of plastic. Plastic is a modern wonder of chemistry. Since its discovery in the 1860s, plastic has revolutionized how many items are made.

Plastics are polymers. Polymer comes from the Greek words *poly* meaning many and *mer* meaning parts. A polymer is a giant molecule, which is really a long chain of molecules connected end to end. As you already learned, many polymers occur naturally, including rubber, wool, silk, and DNA. However **plastic** is a synthetic, or man-made, polymer.

The first artificial polymer was made in 1862. It was called *celluloid* because it was made from the cellulose found in cotton fibers. Later, polymers were made from coal tar. Today, plastic polymers are made from petroleum, or oil. The main ingredient is ethylene (a gas) which is combined with a catalyst that causes the molecules to form long chains. The first petroleum-based plastic was made in 1907. It was called Bakelite and was a dark brown moldable plastic that was mainly used for radio cabinets and later for TV cabinets or cases. Other famous plastics include nylon, which was invented by the DuPont Corporation in 1930, polyester, and acrylic.

One very interesting way that plastic is used is in the making of clothing. Polymer chips are melted. Then the liquid plastic is forced through very tiny holes and drawn into a thread. The thread is very thin and very flexible. This plastic thread is then woven into cloth to be used for clothing and other products. Check the labels of your clothes and see how many of them contain polyester or nylon. Other man-made fibers include acetate and rayon, which are made from cellulose, not from petroleum.

Most plastics fall into two categories. One kind is thermoplastic. **Thermoplastic** is made by melting plastic chips, and then injecting the liquid into

Fun Fact

Some plastics are ten times harder than steel.

a mold. As the plastic cools, it hardens and keeps its form. Thermoplastics will melt again if they are reheated. There are many uses for thermoplastics including trash cans and PVC pipe. However, it is very inconvenient in some uses for plastics to become soft or begin to melt when they become hot. Therefore, scientists have also developed thermosetting resin.

Thermosetting resin melts when it is heated initially. This liquid is placed in a mold under pressure in a process called compression molding. This kind of plastic hardens under pressure. Then once it cools, it will not melt again even if it becomes hot. This is much better for making items like coffee cups and baking dishes. Thermosetting resin is also used for car bodies and boat hulls, as well as a great number of other applications.

Today, millions of tons of plastic are produced each year. And the uses for plastic are innumerable. Plastics are used for counter tops, plastic bowls, and cooking utensils. Plastics are also used in carpet and other floor coverings. Pens, paintbrush handles, and many other art supplies are made from plastic. Plastics are used to make film. Plastics are used for fishing equipment and tricycles. And plastics are even used to make artificial joints for people. These are only a few of the many uses for plastics. If you look around you, you will find that plastics affect every area of your life.

One of the biggest concerns about all of the plastic that is used every day is the fact that plastic does not decompose. Once the plastic is thrown away, it often ends up in a landfill where it will sit for hundreds of years before breaking down. To help reduce this problem, most cities now offer recycling programs. Plastic, glass, metal, paper, and cardboard can all be recycled. While glass, metal, paper, and cardboard have been recycled for decades, recycling of plastics on a large scale is a relatively new idea. Recycling non-plastic

Many everyday items are made from plastic.

materials is relatively easy compared to plastic recycling. Because of the shape of the plastic polymers, it is difficult to break the molecules apart, so different types of plastic cannot easily be recycled together and must be separated from each other.

Most plastic items are stamped with a recycling number which indicates what type of plastic it contains. When items reach a recycling center they must be sorted. In many cases this is done by hand. Workers pull out cardboard, paper, and plastics. The plastics are then sorted by type. The remaining materials are sent on to machines that use magnets to separate steel cans from aluminum cans. Then glass is separated by hand according to the various colors. This is a very labor intensive process, but a load of recyclables is usually processed in about an hour.

To reduce the costs and time required for sorting, companies have been developing better ways to sort recyclables. Many recycling centers now have machines that use spectrophotometry and other scientific principles to automatically separate various materials. These machines shine a halogen light on the materials as they pass by on a conveyor belt. Each type of material reflects back a unique spectrum of infrared light. The computer analyzes this light to determine the size, shape, color, and location of the item as well as what type of plastic, paper, or glass the item is. A jet of air then pushes the item onto the correct conveyor belt. This is a much more efficient way to sort materials.

Most water and soft drink bottles are made from plastic number 1, which is PET (polyethylene terephthalate). This plastic is often recycled into plastic furniture, carpet, tote bags, and other items. Other

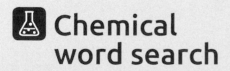

Chemical word search

Using the "Chemical Word Search," review the meaning of each word then find the words in the puzzle.

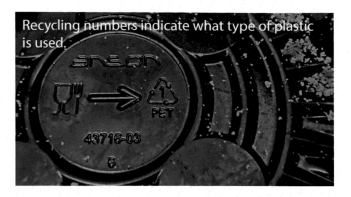

Recycling numbers indicate what type of plastic is used.

bottles and containers are plastic number 2, which is HDPE (high density polyethylene). This type of plastic gets recycled into pens, other bottles, and plastic lumber. For many years these were the only plastics that most recycling programs would accept. However, with improved recycling processes most plastics are now accepted.

Plastic number 4 is found in shopping bags and other plastic bags. These are usually collected separately from other plastics because they tend to get caught in the machinery that separates the other material that has been collected. Plastic 6 is Styrofoam. This type of plastic is very difficult to recycle, and most recycling programs will not accept it.

Although most people would agree that recycling plastic is a good idea, there is still controversy surrounding plastic recycling. Some people argue that the costs involved in collecting, sorting, and recycling outweigh the benefits. Others argue that the methods used to recycle plastics put toxic materials back into the environment. And other people just don't want

to be bothered with sorting their trash before getting rid of it. These issues are all being addressed, and plastic recycling has become much more common in recent years. This means we use less petroleum to make plastic items, and we often use less wood and other materials that those plastic items now replace. So, keep your eyes open for recycled plastic, and see where it shows up around you. ✳

What did we learn?

- What is plastic?
- What was celluloid, the first artificial polymer, made from?
- What is the difference between thermoplastic and thermosetting resin?
- Why are people concerned about throwing plastic items away?
- What does the recycling number on a plastic item mean?
- Why are plastic bags usually recycled separately from other plastics?

🚀 Taking it further

- Name three ways that plastic is used in sports.
- What advantages do plastic items have over natural materials?

Polymer ball

There are many fun experiments that you can perform that involve polymers. Today you will make a polymer bouncy ball.

Purpose: To make a polymer ball

Materials: borax powder, water, plastic zipper bag, two cups, white glue, cornstarch, markers

Procedure:

1. Mix 2 tablespoons of warm water with ½ teaspoon of borax powder in a cup.

2. In a second cup, combine 1 tablespoon of glue, ½ teaspoon of the borax mixture you just made, and

1 tablespoon of cornstarch. Do not stir. Allow the ingredients to react together for 15 seconds.

3. After 15 seconds begin stirring the ingredients together.

4. Once it becomes impossible to stir the mixture, remove it from the cup and roll it between your hands. Continue rolling the ball until most of the stickiness is gone.

5. Decorate your ball with markers.

6. Enjoy bouncing your ball. Store it in a plastic zipper bag to keep it fresh.

32

Fireworks

Is it the fourth of July?

How are fireworks made?

One of the most exciting parts of any Independence Day celebration is watching the fireworks display after the sun goes down. Fireworks have become an American Fourth of July tradition. But the earliest fireworks were the invention of the Chinese in the tenth century. These early fireworks were more like the later Roman Candles and were used in warfare rather than for entertainment. In 1242 an English monk named Roger Bacon wrote down the first European recipe for black powder, a key ingredient in fireworks. Then, in 1353, black powder was used by the Arabs in the first gun. But the first known use of fireworks for entertainment purposes was in France, when Louis XIV amazed his guests with fireworks sometime in the late seventeenth century. Later, the Italians added color to the fireworks and one of the most enjoyable forms of entertainment was born.

Making fireworks is a very specialized and somewhat dangerous use of chemical reactions. The recipe for each firework is unique. Most fireworks companies are family owned and the recipes for their fireworks are strictly guarded secrets, passed down from generation to generation. Still, there are some common steps in making and firing fireworks.

Each fireworks shell is packed with balls of chemicals. How the balls are packed determines how it will explode and what the explosion will look like. Different chemicals emit different colors when burned, so the type of chemical determines the color that will be given off. Sodium gives off a yellow light, copper salt produces blue, lithium and strontium salts produce red, and barium nitrate produces green.

The chemical balls are layered inside the shell and held in place by rice or corn. The shell is then wrapped in brown paper and paste and allowed to dry. Charges of black powder and fuses are then added to the shell. The charge on the bottom lifts the shell into the air. A bursting charge is added as well. Each charge has its own fuse, which determines when it will blow so that the shell does not burst before it reaches an appropriate altitude.

When the bursting charge explodes, the energy released excites the electrons in the outermost shell of the atoms, moving the electrons to a higher

Fun Fact

Fireworks are usually stored in bunkers that are separated by 20-foot mounds of sand. This way if one bunker somehow explodes, the others would still be safe.

Pipes being set up for a fireworks show

One pipe is used for each shell to be fired. Sand is packed around and in between each pipe to hold it in place. An appropriately sized mortar is set in each specific place according to the plan for when each shell is to be fired.

Next, a wire is run from a firing board to each mortar. The wire is then connected to the firing fuse of the shell. The firing board is then used to ignite each shell in the proper order. The size and order of each shell is determined ahead of time to guarantee a spectacular display. ✳

What did we learn?

- What are the key ingredients in a fireworks shell?
- Why does a fireworks shell have two different black powder charges?
- How do fireworks generate flashes of light?
- What determines the color of the firework?

Taking it further

- How can a firework explode with one color and then change to a different color?
- Why would employees at a fireworks plant have to wear only cotton clothing?

energy level than they would normally be in. This is an unstable situation so the electrons quickly go back to their original energy level. When the electrons return to their normal energy levels, they release energy in the form of light. Different chemical compounds release different wavelengths of light, thus we enjoy a wide variety of different colors of fireworks.

Nearly as much work goes into setting up a fireworks display as goes into making the shells. It can take up to two days to set up everything for a 30–60 minute fireworks show. First, copper pipes are used as mortars for firing the larger shells and PVC pipes are used to hold the smaller shells.

Designing a fireworks display

Each firework has a special design to give just the desired effect. You can design your own fireworks display by making a fireworks picture. Decide the shapes and colors of the exploding fireworks and then draw the shapes on a piece of construction paper with glue. Next, sprinkle colored glitter on the glue and allow it to dry. Be creative and design fireworks that you would like to see.

Colored flames

You can experience different colored flames in your own campfire. You can soak pinecones in different chemical solutions. When they are dry you can burn them in a campfire. They will burn with different colors of flame because of the different chemicals they are coated with.

Purpose: To observe the different colors produced by different salts

Materials: pinecones, container, water, as many of the chemicals in the chart as you can obtain

Procedure:

For each color you wish to produce:

1. Dissolve as much of the colorant chemical as you can dissolve in 2 cups of water. It is okay if some chemical settles to the bottom of the container.

2. Place a pinecone in the solution and allow it to soak for several hours.

3. Remove the pinecone and allow it to completely dry. It is then ready to burn.

4. **Adult supervision is required for this step.** Burn your pinecones in a safe area, where there is no danger of catching anything else on fire. Do not cook food over the pinecones. The different colored flames are beautiful to watch but could make your food toxic.

Color	Chemical
Orange	Calcium Chloride (a bleaching powder)
Yellow	Sodium Chloride (table salt)
Yellowish Green	Borax
Green	Copper Sulfate
Blue	Copper Chloride
Purple	Potassium Chloride
White	Magnesium Sulfate (Epsom salts)

33

Rocket Fuel

Do you need a
rocket scientist?

What is rocket fuel made from?

Words to know:

Newton's third law of motion

Challenge words:

solid rocket fuel   hypergolic fuel

cryogenic fuel

Have you ever watched a spacecraft lift off and fly into space? The engines ignite, and steam and fire billow out the bottom as the spacecraft lifts off the ground, picking up speed every second. This is an exciting thing to watch. And a lot of chemistry went into making the rocket fuel needed for that exciting liftoff.

Combustion is a chemical reaction that produces large amounts of heat. This reaction is what provides the thrust that pushes the rocket off the ground. In most modern rockets, the fuel of choice is the combination of liquid oxygen and liquid hydrogen. These two elements are kept under pressure and then combined in a combustion reaction inside the rocket engine. At very high temperatures the oxygen and hydrogen combust and turn into steam. The resulting gases are forced out the back of the rocket engine at very high speeds. The water molecules travel at about 1,250 miles per hour (560 meters/second). But not all of the hydrogen and oxygen atoms combine to form water; some atoms just evaporate and then leave the engine at high speeds, providing additional thrust. The O_2 molecules travel at up to 950 mph (425 m/s) and the hydrogen atoms move at up to 3,580 mph (1600 m/s).

Newton's third law of motion states that for every action there is an equal and opposite reaction. So, as the gases escape out the back of the rocket

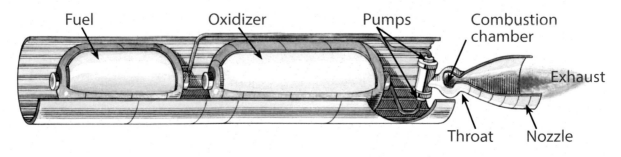

Fuel   Oxidizer   Pumps   Combustion chamber

Exhaust

Throat   Nozzle

one of the first rocket fuels. The gas produced in the combustion of kerosene is carbon dioxide. Carbon dioxide is heavier than steam so it does not move as quickly, thus it produces less thrust. Therefore, oxygen and hydrogen are more efficient rocket fuels.

The next time you see a video of the space shuttle or other rocket taking off, remember that the white clouds that are billowing around the rocket are not smoke as you might think, but actually clouds of steam from the oxygen/hydrogen reaction. ✷

What did we learn?

- What is combustion?
- What two elements are combined in most modern rocket fuel?
- What compound is produced in this reaction?
- How does combining oxygen and hydrogen produce lift?
- What is Newton's third law of motion?

Taking it further

- Why is oxygen and hydrogen a better choice for rocket fuel than kerosene was?

engine, they are pushing the rocket forward with the same amount of thrust. This is the basic physics behind a rocket.

Not all of the liquid hydrogen is used in the combustion reaction. Because the reaction produces so much heat, some of the liquid hydrogen is piped around the inside of the engine where it absorbs heat to keep the parts from melting.

Earlier rocket engines did not use liquid hydrogen and liquid oxygen as their propellants. Kerosene was

Balloon rocket

Purpose: To learn how rockets work

Materials: balloon, straw, string, tape, two chairs

Procedure:

1. Blow up a balloon and then release it. What happens? Tape a straw to the balloon.

2. Thread a string through the straw.

3. Tape the ends of the string to opposite walls of a room or to two chairs that are several feet apart.

4. Blow up the balloon and pull it to one end of the string.

5. Release the balloon.

Conclusion: When you first released the balloon, it flew around the room. This is because the air molecules inside the balloon were forced out the end. And as we already learned about motion, for every action there is an equal and opposite reaction. So, as the air molecules rushed out the back of the balloon they produced a force on the front of the balloon that made it move.

The string provided a guidance system for the rocket, and the balloon should have flown forward along the string.

A real rocket has a very exact engine that carefully controls how the molecules exit the engine so that the rocket lifts off straight and does not fly all over the place like your balloon did.

🏅 Fuel types

Although most modern rockets use the combustion of liquid hydrogen and liquid oxygen as their propellant, there are actually three different categories of rocket fuel that are used for different purposes.

First there are **solid rocket fuel** engines. A solid rocket fuel begins with a combustible material. Originally, gunpowder was used as the fuel for rockets, but modern rockets use fuels with more energy. This fuel is bound together with an oxidizer, which is a chemical that provides the necessary oxygen for combustion. The fuel and oxidizer are formed into grains which are compressed to form the core of the engine. Solid rocket fuel is usually ignited by an electrical charge.

Solid rocket fuel is not used in most space rockets, but is commonly used for model rockets. Also, because solid rocket fuel can be stored for indefinite periods of time, many military missiles use solid rocket fuel.

The most common type of rocket fuel is **cryogenic fuel**. Cryogenic fuel must be stored under very high pressure and at very low temperatures. This is the type of liquid fuel discussed earlier in the lesson. Hydrogen, which is the fuel, and oxygen, which is the oxidizer, are stored under great pressure and then released at a specific rate into the combustion chamber where they are burned. This type of engine is more complicated than a solid rocket engine, but it allows for more control of the rate at which the propellants are burned. A solid rocket engine must continue burning until all of the fuel is used up, but a liquid fuel engine can be turned on and off.

A third type of fuel is called **hypergolic fuel**. Hypergolic refers to two substances that ignite when they come in contact with each other. Hypergolic fuel rockets can be controlled the same way as a hydrogen/oxygen engine; however, they produce more toxic chemicals in their combustion reaction. Therefore, they are used only in a few types of rockets.

34

Fun with Chemistry: Final Project

Understanding chemical reactions

Have fun with chemical reactions.

Now that you have learned about atoms and molecules, you should have a better understanding of what happens during chemical reactions. Take a few minutes to review what you have learned. Especially review lessons 17–20 on chemical reactions. Now, let's have some fun!

🧠 What did we learn?

- What was your favorite chemical reaction?
- Why did you like that reaction?

🚀 Taking it further

- What do you think will happen if you use skim milk in the first activity?
- What colors would you expect to see separate out of orange ink? Brown ink?
- Why is it important not to inhale the sodium polyacrylate from the diaper?

Fun chemical reactions

For each activity, complete the appropriate section of the "Fun With Chemistry" worksheet.

Older students should make a hypothesis about what they expect to see in each experiment before performing the experiment.

Purpose: To experiment with various chemical reactions

Materials: "Fun with Chemistry" worksheet, milk, dish, food coloring, water, sink, liquid dish soap, paper towel, markers, unused disposable diaper, scissors, large glass, eye-dropper, white glue, liquid starch, plastic zipper bag

Activity 1—Moving molecules

Procedure:

1. Pour one cup of milk into a dish.

2. Place a drop of blue food coloring, red food coloring, and green food coloring equally spaced around the edge of the dish.

3. Observe the movement of the colors for several seconds.

4. Now add a drop of liquid dish soap to the center of the milk and watch the movement of the colors. Write your observations and explanation on the worksheet.

Activity 2—More moving molecules

Procedure:

1. Fold a paper towel in half.

2. Using a black water-soluble marker, draw a 1-inch wide bar about one inch from the narrow edge of the paper.

3. Draw a green bar and other colors of bars also one inch from the edge. Make sure none of your bars touch each other.

4. Put about ½ inch of water in a sink.

5. Carefully place the edge of the paper towel in the water so the bars are just above the water level.

6. Set the paper towel against the edge of the sink and place a heavy object on the top edge to hold it in place.

7. Allow the water to slowly wick up the paper towel for one hour.

8. Observe the ink after one hour.

9. Remove the paper from the water and allow it to dry. What did you observe about the ink? Write your observations on the worksheet.

Activity 3—Super absorbent molecules

You will be removing the powder that is found in an unused disposable baby diaper. **During this activity be very careful not to inhale or swallow any of the powder, and be careful not to get it in your eyes.**

Procedure:

1. Cut away the plastic outer covering of a disposable diaper.

2. Carefully place a large section of the inner padding in a plastic zipper bag.

3. Wash your hands and seal the bag.

4. Hold the padding toward the top of the bag and shake until you have about ½–1 teaspoon of powder in the bottom of the bag.

5. Carefully remove the padding and discard it. Again, wash your hands.

6. Carefully pour the powder into in a large glass or mixing bowl.

7. In a separate cup, combine one cup of water and a few drops of food coloring.

8. Using an eyedropper, add the colored water one drop at a time to the powder. What do you see happening?

9. After adding several droppers of water, begin adding water 1 teaspoon at a time. How much water do you predict the powder/gel will be able to absorb? See if you can add the whole cup of water to the gel. Write your observations on the worksheet.

Activity 4—Making your own goop

Procedure:

1. Pour ½ cup of white glue into a mixing bowl.

2. Add a few drops of food coloring and stir in the food coloring until it is well mixed.

3. Slowly add ¼ to ½ cup of liquid starch to the glue, mixing well until you have a gooey mixture that is easy to handle. What do you see happening? You can play with your goop.

4. When you are done, place the goop in a plastic zipper bag for later playing.

5. Wash your hands and record your observations on the worksheet.

Explanation for each activity

Activity 1—Moving molecules

Milk is a colloid, a liquid with solids suspended in it. Most of the solids in milk are fat molecules. These fat molecules keep the food coloring molecules separated from each other for the most part. When you add the soap, the soap molecules attract the fat molecules, allowing the food coloring to dissolve in the milk.

Activity 2—More moving molecules

This is an activity called chromatography. Black, green, and many other colors of ink are a combination of different colored ink molecules. These different molecules have different weights so they move up the paper towel at different rates. This allows you to see the different colors of molecules in the ink.

Activity 3—Super absorbent molecules

The powder in disposable diapers is a polymer called sodium polyacrylate. These molecules have the ability to absorb over 100 times their weight in water. This makes it very useful for diapers. This chemical is also used as a soil additive for some potted plants. These molecules absorb the water and then slowly release it, allowing you to water your plants less often, and to use less water.

Activity 4—Making your own goop

Starch and glue molecules combine to form a polymer. Recall that a polymer is a long flexible chain of molecules. This flexibility is what makes the goop so much fun.

⊛ More experiments

There are many more fun chemistry experiments on the Internet. Choose one that sounds interesting and perform it. Always obtain permission from your parent or teacher before conducting your own experiment.

35

Conclusion

Appreciating our orderly universe

Thank God for His amazing universe!

We live in a world that operates according to specific natural laws that were set in motion by God. We have learned how God designed our world to recycle all of the elements so that the matter in the universe is not used up. God designed our bodies to perform chemical reactions that are complementary to the reactions performed by plants; plants provide food and oxygen for us, and we provide carbon dioxide for photosynthesis.

All that you have learned about chemistry should point out that God is the master designer of our world. Read some Scripture verses that describe God's work in our world. Read Psalm 148, Isaiah 42:5–7, Colossians 1:16–17, and Job 42:1–2.

Now take a few moments and thank God for creating a world that obeys His rules, even at the molecular and atomic levels. ✳

Glossary

Acid   Substance the easily forms hydronium ions by producing H+ ions in water

Acid salt   Salt formed when there is more acid than base

Activation energy   The energy required for a chemical reaction to take place

Alloy   Resultant metal when a small amount of one metal is added to another

Anesthetic   Chemical that stops or blocks pain

Antibiotic   Substance produced by living organisms to kill bacteria

Aromatic   Smell is easily detected

Atomic mass unit/amu   Mass of a proton or neutron

Atomic mass/Mass number   Number of protons plus the number of neutrons in an atom

Atomic number   Number of protons in an atom

Atom/Element   Smallest part of matter that cannot be broken down by ordinary chemical means

Base   Substance that easily forms hydroxide ions

Basic salt   Salt formed when there is more base than acid

Carbon cycle   Recycling of carbon for reuse by plants and animals

Catalyst   Substance that increases the reaction rate by lowering activation energy

Ceramic   Inorganic nonmetallic material formed by the action of heat

Chemical analysis   Use of chemical reactions to determine what a substance is made of

Chemical equations   Symbolic representation of a chemical reaction

Chemical formula   Symbolic representation of the atoms in a molecule

Chemical reaction   Occurs when atomic bonds are formed or broken

Chemistry   Study of the basic building blocks of matter

Chemists   Scientists who study how matter reacts to other matter

Composition reaction   Two or more atoms combine to form a molecule

Compound   Bonding of two or more different kinds of atoms

Covalent bonding   Molecules formed by sharing of electrons

Crop rotation   System of growing different crops each season to replace nutrients in soil

Crystal   Substance whose atoms form in an orderly pattern

Decomposers   Organisms that break down dead plant and animal cells into simple chemical compounds

Decomposition reaction   A molecule breaks apart into two or more atoms

Decomposition   Process that breaks down dead cells to recycle chemicals

Dehydrogenation   Removal of hydrogen atoms from a molecule

Diatomic molecule   Two of the same type of atom bonded together

Ductile   Able to be drawn into a wire

Edge   Where two faces of a crystal meet

Electrolysis   Separating of atoms by passing electrical current through them

Electron energy levels   The various distances at which an electron orbits the nucleus of an atom

Electronegativity   A measure of how strongly an element attracts electrons to itself

Electrons   Negatively charged particles orbiting the nucleus of an atom

Endothermic reaction   Reaction in which energy is stored

Enzyme   Catalyst involved in biological functions

Ethnobotanist   Person who studies plants to develop new medicines

Exothermic reaction   Reaction in which energy is released

Face   Flat surface of a crystal

Fallow   Not planting any crops for one or more years

Family   Column of the periodic table

Fertilizer   Chemicals added to make soil more productive

First law of thermodynamics   Matter and energy cannot be created or destroyed; they can only change forms

Free electron model   Metals share electrons on a large scale

Fungicide   Chemical that kills fungus

Genetic engineering/Genetic modification   Manipulation of a plant's or animal's genes to produce offspring with desired characteristics

Halogens   Top four elements in column VIIA on the periodic table

Healing herbs   Plants used as cures for illnesses

Herbicide   Chemical that kills unwanted plants

High electronegativity   An element does not easily give up its electrons

Hydrogenation   Addition of hydrogen atoms to a molecule

Hydronium ion   Water molecule that has reacted with an H^+ ion

Hydroponics   Growth of plants without soil

Hydroxide ion OH^- ion

Indicator   Substance that changes color when it reacts with a particular chemical

Inert   Non-reactive

Inhibitor   Substance the slows down the reaction rate

Ionic bond/Ionic bonding   A bond formed by transferring of electrons

Ionic compound   Molecules formed by ionic bonding

Ion   An element with an electrical charge due to missing or extra electrons

Latex   Sticky, milky substance found in rubber trees

Low electronegativity   An element easily gives up its electrons

Malleable   Able to be hammered into a shape

Matter   Anything that has mass and takes up space

Metallic bonding   Substance formed when thousands of atoms freely share their electrons

Metalloids/Semi-conductors   Elements on the periodic table between the metals and nonmetals

Molecule   Group of chemically connected atoms

Neutrons   Electrically neutral particles in the nucleus of an atom

Noble gases   Elements in column VIIIA, non-reactive elements

Normal salt   Salt formed when an acid and base completely neutralize each other

Nucleus   Tight mass of protons and neutrons in the center of an atom

Organic farming   Growing plants without the use of artificial chemicals

Oxidation   Adding of oxygen to a molecule

Period   Row of the periodic table

Perfume   Liquid with a pleasant smell

Pesticide   Chemical that kills unwanted insects

Pharmaceuticals/Medicines   Chemicals used to cure illnesses

pH scale   Indicates the strength of an acid or base

Plastic   Substance made from polymers formed from petroleum

Polymers   Long chains of molecules connected end to end

Products   Atoms or molecules formed by a chemical reaction

Proteins, fats, and carbohydrates   Main chemicals used by the body

Proton   Positively charged particle in the nucleus of an atom

Reactants   Atoms or molecules present at the beginning of a chemical reaction

Reaction rate   The rate or speed at which a chemical reaction takes place

Reactive   Easily combines chemically with other elements

Reduction   Removal of oxygen from a molecule

Rubber   Flexible substance made from latex

Salt   Substance formed when an acid and a base combine

Scavenger   Animal that eats dead animals

Smelting   Refining ore through high temperatures

Solvent   Substance used to dissolve other substances

Solvent extraction   Removing of scent molecules by a solvent

Steam distillation   Use of steam to vaporize scent molecules

Synthetic   Man-made, not naturally occurring

Thermoplastic   Plastic that can be melted over and over again

Thermosetting resin   Plastic that will not melt after it initially cools and hardens

Third law of motion   For every action there is an equal and opposite reaction

Transition elements   Elements in the center columns, labeled with the letter B

Vaccination/Vaccine   Chemical solution that stimulates your body's immune system against a particular disease

Valence electrons   Electrons in outermost energy level of an atom

Vulcanization   Use of sulfur to make rubber elastic in all temperatures

Challenge Glossary

Acid/base titration   Method for determining the unknown quantity of a base (or acid) by carefully measuring the exact amount of acid (or base) needed to completely neutralize it

Active ceramic   Bioceramic that chemically reacts with tissues in the body

Allotrope   Different forms or molecules made from the same element

Anhydrous   Substance that has had the water removed

Anion   Negatively charged ion

Bioceramic   Ceramic that is used in the body

Buckminsterfullerene/Buckyball   Carbon atom in the shape of a soccer ball

Carbon nanotube   Extremely tiny thread-like tube created from matrix of carbon atoms

Casein   Polymer found in cow's milk

Cation   Positively charged ion

Chemotherapy   Use of chemicals to treat cancer

Cryogenic rocket fuel   Liquid fuel stored under pressure at very low temperatures

Dehydration   The process of removing water

Double displacement reaction   Reaction in which two substance trade places

Electroplating   Depositing a thin layer of metal on a conductor using electricity

Enthalpy   Energy stored in a molecule's bonds

Heterogeneous catalyst   Catalyst in a different phase from the reactants

Homogeneous catalyst   Catalyst in the same phase as the reactants

Hydrated   Bonded with water

Hydrate   Crystalline substance that is bonded with water

Hydrogen fuel cell   Technology that combines hydrogen and oxygen to produce electricity

Hypergolic rocket fuel   Liquid fuel that combusts when two substances come in contact with each other

Inert ceramic   Ceramic that does not react with the body

Isotope   Same type of atom with different numbers of neutrons

Keratin   Polymer found in animal horns and human hair and nails

Lac   Polymer produced in the insect called a lac

Nanotechnology   The manipulation of matter on the atomic or molecular level for technological uses

Neutralize   To make an acid of base chemically neutral

Noble metals   Those that do not easily react with other metals

Poor metals   Those to the right of the transition metals, between transition metals and metalloids

Protease   Enzyme that breaks down proteins

Proton acceptor   Alternate definition of a base when the molecule accepts a proton ion

Proton donor   Alternate definition of an acid when the molecule donates a proton ion

Quantitative measurement   One in which actual numbers are used

Reactivity series   List of metals from most to least reactive

Resorbable ceramic   Bioceramic that breaks down inside the body

Rosin   Polymer found in dead wood and wood pulp

Silk   A polymer produced by silk worms

Single displacement reaction   Reaction in which one substance take the place of another

Solid rocket fuel   Rocket fuel bound with an oxidizer in solid form

Super alloy   Alloy that is strong even at high temperatures

Valence   Number of electrons an element needs to lose or gain to be stable

Water of crystallization   Water that is bonded in a hydrate

Index

Photo Credits

3 © Galyna Andrushko | Dreamstime.com
5 Getty Images/iStockphoto
7 ©2008 Jupterimages Corporation
8 ©2008 Jupterimages Corporation
9 ©Richard Lawrence
10 Getty Images/iStockphoto
11 Public domain
13 Getty Images/iStockphoto
15 Public domain
17T ©istockphoto.com/dra_schwartz
17B Public domain
18T ©2008 Jupterimages Corporation
18B Getty Images/Creatas RF
20 ©2008 Jupterimages Corporation
21 Getty Images/iStockphoto
25 Public domain
26 ©2008 Jupterimages Corporation
27 Getty Images/iStockphoto
29 ©2008 Jupterimages Corporation
30T Getty Images/iStockphoto
30B ©Phillip Lawrence
31 Getty Images/iStockphoto
32 ©istockphoto.com/Elke Dennis
34L © Richard Lawrence
34R Creative Commons | Sludge G
35 Getty Images/iStockphoto
37LT Getty Images/Zoonar RF
37LB Getty Images/iStockphoto
37R Getty Images/iStockphoto
38T ©istockphoto.com/Matthew Hull
38B Public Domain
40 ©Phillip Lawrence
41 Getty Images/Stockbyte
42T Getty Images/Hemera
42B Public Domain
46 ©Richard Lawrence
45 ©istockphoto.com/Nancy Nehring
46 ©2008 Jupterimages Corporation

49 ©2008 Jupterimages Corporation
51 ©2008 Jupterimages Corporation
52L ©2008 Answers in Genesis
52R ©2008 Jupterimages Corporation
53 © Richard Lawrence
54 Public domain
56T Getty Images/iStockphoto
56B Getty Images/Stockbyte
57 ©2008 Jupterimages Corporation
60T Getty Images/iStockphoto
60B ©2008 Jupterimages Corporation
61 ©2008 Jupterimages Corporation
63 Getty Images/iStockphoto
64T Getty Images/iStockphoto
64B ©Richard Lawrence
68T Getty Images/iStockphoto
68B ©Richard Lawrence
71 Getty Images/iStockphoto
74 ©2008 Jupterimages Corporation
76 ©2008 Jupterimages Corporation
77 Getty Images
78T Getty Images/iStockphoto
78B ©Tommounsey | Dreamstime.com
79 ©Sudo | Dreamstime.com
81 ©2008 Jupterimages Corporation
82 Getty Images/iStockphoto
83 ©Phillip Lawrence
84 ©2008 Jupterimages Corporation
85 Getty Images/iStockphoto
87T ©2008 Jupterimages Corporation
87B ©Kivig | Dreamstime.com
88 ©2008 Jupterimages Corporation
90 ©Richard Lawrence
91 ©2008 Answers in Genesis
92 ©2008 Jupterimages Corporation
93T Getty Images/Photodisc
93B Getty Images/Fuse
94 Getty Images/Hemera

96 ©2008 Jupterimages Corporation
97T Getty Images/iStockphoto
97B Getty Images/iStockphoto
98 ©2015 Answers in Genesis
99 ©Lockstockbob | Dreamstime.com
100T Getty Images/iStockphoto
100B Getty Images/Zoonar RF
103 ©2008 Jupterimages Corporation
104T Courtesy USDA
104B ©2008 Jupterimages Corporation
105 Getty Images/iStockphoto
106 Public domain
107 © Tine Grebenc | Dreamstime.com
108 Getty Images/iStockphoto
109T Getty Images/iStockphoto
109B ©istockphoto.com/kemie
110 Creative Commons | Izmaelt
111 Getty Images/iStockphoto
112T ©2008 Jupterimages Corporation
112B ©Highlanderimages | Dreamstime.com
113 ©2008 Jupterimages Corporation
115L ©Seesea | Dreamstime.com
115 RT Getty Images/Goodshoot RF
115RB Getty Images/iStockphoto
116 Public domain
118 ©2008 Jupterimages Corporation
119 Public domain
120 Creative Commons | Woakamkurhram
121 ©2008 Jupterimages Corporation
122 ©Mhryciw | Dreamstime.com
124T ©istockphoto.com/Dennis Sabo
124B Getty Images/Dorling Kindersley RF
125 Getty Images/iStockphoto
127 Getty Images/iStockphoto
130 Credit NASA/JPL-Caltech, D. Figer